Goody Two Shoes

A Pantomime

Paul Reakes

A Samuel French Acting Edition

SAMUEL FRENCH

FOUNDED 1830

SAMUELFRENCH.COM
SAMUELFRENCH-LONDON.CO.UK

FOR PRODUCTION ENQUIRIES

UNITED STATES AND CANADA

Info@SamuelFrench.com

1-866-598-8449

UNITED KINGDOM AND EUROPE

Theatre@SamuelFrench-London.co.uk

020-7255-4302

Each title is subject to availability from Samuel French, depending upon country
of performance. Please be aware that GOODY TWO SHOES may not be licensed
by Samuel French in your territory. Professional and amateur producers should
contact the nearest Samuel French office or licensing partner to verify availability.

MUSIC USE NOTE

Licensees are solely responsible for obtaining formal written permission from copyright owners to use copyrighted music in the performance of this play and are strongly cautioned to do so. If no such permission is obtained by the licensee, then the licensee must use only original music that the licensee owns and controls. Licensees are solely responsible and liable for all music clearances and shall indemnify the copyright owners of the play(s) and their licensing agent, Samuel French, against any costs, expenses, losses and liabilities arising from the use of music by licensees. Please contact the appropriate music licensing authority in your territory for the rights to any incidental music.

IMPORTANT BILLING AND CREDIT REQUIREMENTS

If you have obtained performance rights to this title, please refer to your licensing agreement for important billing and credit requirements.

GOODY TWO SHOES

First presented by the Timsbury Theatre Group at the Conygre Hall, Timsbury, Somerset, with the following cast:

Molly Coddle	Dennis Glover
Goody	Tammy Clark
Teddy	Ian Clark
Septica	Anne Colbourne
Rolo	Peter Buchanan
Polo	Patrick Bridges
Simon	Ellie Jordan
Titus Tightwad	John Ford
Cissie	Madeline Stephens
The Elf Cobbler	John Hopper

Directed by **Dennis Jones**
Musical Director **Susan Suart**
Technical Director **Jeff Sluggett**

CHARACTERS

Molly Coddle
Goody, her daughter
Teddy, her son
Septica, an evil sorceress
Rolo⎫
Polo⎭ Septica's servants
Simon
Titus Tightwad, a miserly landlord
Cissie, his niece
The Elf Cobbler
Chorus of Villagers and **Forest Demons**

SYNOPSIS OF SCENES

ACT I
SCENE 1 The Fearsome Forest
SCENE 2 Near the village
SCENE 3 Outside Molly's cottage

ACT II
SCENE 1 Near the village
SCENE 2 Outside Molly's cottage
SCENE 3 Near the village
SCENE 4 The Fearsome Forest
SCENE 5 Before the party
SCENE 6 The Grand Finale

MUSICAL NUMBERS

ACT I

No 1	Song and Dance	Forest Demons
No 2	Comedy song and Dance	Teddy, Molly and Demons
No 3	Song and Dance	Goody and Villagers
No 4	Romantic Duet	Simon and Goody
No 4a	Reprise of Song 1	Forest Demons
No 5	Song and Dance	Cissie and Villagers
No 6	Song and Dance	The Villagers
No 7	Song and Dance	Principals and Villagers
No 8	Song and Dance	Cissie, Simon and Villagers

ACT II

No 9	Song and Dance	Molly, Teddy and Villagers
No 10	Song	Goody
No 10a	Reprise of Song 10	Goody and Villagers
No 11	Comedy Duet	Teddy and Cissie
No 11a	Reprise of Song 1	The Forest Demons
No 12	Song	Simon
No 13	Song and Dance	All
No 14	House Song	Teddy, Rolo, Polo and Audience
No 15	Finale Song or Reprise	All

CHARACTERS AND COSTUMES

Molly Coddle (Dame) is a poor widow, who enjoys both mirth and misery. At times she can be overbearing and brash, but you can't help liking the old girl. After all, she does have rent problems, and the hapless Teddy for a son! She is always on friendly and confidential terms with the audience, and never misses an opportunity of involving them. All her "Panto poor" costumes should be outrageous and comical, with hairdos and make-up to match. Special finale costume.

Goody (Principal Girl) is her daughter. We should take this beautiful young woman to our hearts from the first moment we set eyes on her. She is charm itself, and is never soppy or simpering. Her only fault is trying on a particularly nice pair of shoes, and innocently taking them home with her. If only she knew! A good singing voice and dancing ability is called for. Some emotional acting is required when she loses the love of her life. She looks delightful in all her "Panto poor" costumes. Special finale costume.

Teddy is Molly's son. He is a lovable young buffoon, who soon becomes a favourite with the audience, especially the youngsters. He is not overburdened with brains, and his silly antics and gormless remarks are a constant irritation to his mum. He also has the misfortune to fall for the awful Cissie! He is involved in plenty of comic business and audience participation. Singing and dancing ability would be an advantage. All his "Panto poor" costumes are comically tatty and ill-fitting. Special finale costume.

Septica is an evil sorceress. She is permanently bad-tempered and morose. This is not helped by the uncomfortable shoes she has to wear while waiting for her "comfy" ones to be repaired. When she discovers that her precious footwear has been stolen, she really hits the roof! No-one is safe from her wrath, and she relishes the thought of punishing the thief. She never misses the opportunity of goading the audience into a frenzy of boos and hisses. She is the one we all love to hate. Her costumes, headgear and make-up should be bizarre and magnificently evil.

Rolo and **Polo** are her servants. They are a very likeable pair, involved in plenty of comic business and audience participation. Polo is the dopey one. Although terrified of Septica, they try to outwit her evil plans for Goody. They are written be played as a male duo, but can be a male and female, or an all-female partnership if desired. Singing and dancing ability is not essential. As they are servants to an evil Sorceress, they wear suitably bizarre outfits. Polo's is ill-fitting and looks extremely comical.

Simon (Principal Boy) is the young man whose love life is turned upside-down by the magic shoes. Under their influence, he first falls in love with Goody, then with Cissie, and then with Goody again! Each time it happens he is thoroughly convinced that he is truly in love with the right girl. He is handsome and dashing, with a flashing smile and a very nice pair of legs. A good singing voice and dancing ability is called for. His costumes are attractive without being elaborate. Special finale costume.

Titus Tightwad is the miserly landlord. He is not really a villain, just a mean, grasping old skinflint. In the best traditions of melodrama, he threatens to evict Molly from her cottage if she can't pay the rent. Like everyone else, he cannot stand his awful niece Cissie. He only tolerates her because of the large fortune she will one day inherit. Singing and dancing ability is not essential. Ideally, he should be thin and wizened in appearance. His black frockcoat and top hat, bought many years ago to last, are now very worn and threadbare.

Cissie is his niece. She is an obnoxious spoilt brat, with a very pronounced "lithp". She is probably in her late teens or early twenties (but can be older) but still uses the mannerisms and voice of a little girl. She thinks this makes her "cute and adorable", which of course it doesn't! She also believes that she is far superior to anyone else. This makes her very unpopular with the audience, especially the youngsters. Singing and dancing ability is an advantage. And she still dresses like a little girl! Short frilly frocks with lots of fancy bows, etc. Ringlets, ribbons and white ankle socks complete the nauseating picture! She also gets to wear a ludicrous hat. Finale costume.

The Elf Cobbler is somewhere between a pixie and a gnome. A wispy little fellow with pointed ears, a turned-up nose, and a small beard. He is proud of his workmanship, terrified of the evil sorceress, and quite devious when it comes to saving the day. A short male performer is preferable, but the part can be played by a female or a competent youngster. Singing and dancing ability is not called for. His costume and make-up can be straight out of a traditional fairy storybook, or something of your own devising. A short apron with a pocket is essential.

The Chorus, Dancers and Children appear as the Forest Demons (large and small), and as the Villagers. There are several small speaking parts required for the Villagers. Their costumes are of the picturesque peasant variety. The outfits and make-up for the Demons should create a bizarre collection of monsters: some are small and goblin-like, others sinuous and agile, others huge, hairy and lumbering: in fact, something to suit all ages of your Chorus and Dancers!

PRODUCTION NOTES

STAGING

The pantomime offers opportunities for elaborate staging, but can be produced quite simply if funds and facilities are limited.

There are two full sets:
> The Fearsome Forest
> Outside Molly's cottage

These scenes are interlinked with tabs or one frontcloth scene:
> Near the village

There can be a special Finale setting, or the Forest scene can be used with the addition of a triumphal arch and flower garlands, etc.

The Fearsome Forest
This is the classic "spooky" forest of fairytales. It is full of gnarled and twisted trees, with branches that reach out like bony arms and fingers. Some of the trunks appear to have distorted and grotesque faces in them. There is also an abundance of tangled undergrowth and curling creepers. DR, a larger tree is the home and workshop of the Elf Cobbler. In its trunk there is a concealed door. This should not be too large, and completely undetectable when closed. At one point the door opens magically by itself. As several of the characters enter and exit from the tree, some careful masking will be required.

Outside Molly's cottage

This setting represents a quaint village with thatched cottages, duck pond and village green, etc. Molly's cottage, with practical front door, needs to be only partially seen.

Near the Village

This is a well-painted frontcloth representing a country road with the village in the distance.

LIGHTING AND EFFECTS

Really eerie lighting is required for the opening of the two forest scenes. This should be accompanied by weird sounds, and some well-controlled ground mist. In each case, after the Demon's musical number, the general lighting becomes brighter, but it must still retain a spooky atmosphere. General lighting for the Village scenes should be bright and sunny. A special magical effect is required for when the person wearing the magic shoes makes a wish. Whenever Goody does this she is totally unaware of what she is doing. On these occasions the magical effect should be noticeable, but in no way forbidding or frightening. It should just be a fairly brief and unusual change in the general lighting, accompanied by a distant magical tinkling sound. However, when Cissie makes her wish things are very different and lasts a while longer! The lighting becomes dark and sinister. Perhaps a few flashes of lightning and rolls of thunder. Strange, unearthly sounds fill the air. When Septica is about to cast her evil spell to destroy the others, there is more sinister lighting, thunder, lightning, and eerie noises. This ends in a blinding flash, followed by a complete black-out. A flickering light effect is required for the "silent film" sequence at the beginning of Act II. An offstage microphone is required for when the Elf Cobbler is talking from inside his tree. Extra use of follow spots for entrances and musical numbers, etc. are at the director's discretion.

THE SILENT FILM SEQUENCE

This opens Act II, Scene 1. The stage directions in the script are only suggestions. Individual directors will have their own ideas of how to present the sequence. As in the days of the silent cinema, the characters express their emotions with exaggerated gestures. These need to be even more exaggerated for maximum comedy effect. The action should be accompanied by suitable mood music, played on a piano. The cinematic effect can be achieved simply by the use of a flickering light (not strobe.)

If back-projection facilities are available, the whole sequence could be pre-filmed and shown on a screen!

THE MAGIC SHOES

These need to be striking and distinctive in appearance. I would suggest that you use a plain court shoe, sprayed with glitter and decorated with fancy buckles or bows. The story calls for two pairs of identical magic shoes. One pair belongs to Septica, the evil sorceress. The second pair are cunningly used by the Elf Cobbler to bring about Septica's downfall. Unless your female performers take the same size, it will be necessary to replicate the shoes. After all, we don't want your cast to suffer too much for their art!

Paul Reakes

Other works by Paul Reakes
published by Samuel French Ltd

Pantomimes

Babes in the Wood
Bluebeard
Dick Turpin
King Arthur
King Humpty Dumpty
Little Jack Horner
Little Miss Muffet
Little Red Riding Hood
Little Tommy Tucker
Old Mother Hubbard
Robinson Crusoe and the Pirates
Santa in Space
Sinbad the Sailor

Plays

Bang, You're Dead!
Mantrap

ACT I
SCENE 1

The Fearsome Forest

This is a weird and sinister-looking place with gnarled and twisted trees at the back and sides. Strange vegetation and curling creepers abound. Prominent R *is a larger tree with a concealed door in its trunk. This is the home and workshop of the Elf Cobbler*

When the CURTAIN *rises, the stage is empty. The lighting is spooky and there are eerie sounds and ground mist*

To suitable creepy music, the grotesque Forest Demons, large and small, emerge from behind the trees. They go into their bizarre song and dance

Song 1

After the number, the Demons drift into the background, and exit

Rolo creeps on cautiously L. *He stops* C *to look about him*

Polo creeps on backwards L

Polo backs into Rolo, and they both yell with fright. After sorting themselves out, Polo goes up to search among the trees L. *Rolo is about to do the same on the other side, when he suddenly catches sight of the audience*

Rolo (*attracting Polo's attention*) Psst! *Psst!*
Polo (*peering out from behind a tree*) Who was that?
Rolo Me. Come here.
Polo (*scuttling down to him*) What is it?
Rolo Don't look now, but we're being ogled.
Polo Cor! I never felt a thing!
Rolo (*pointing to the audience*) Look!
Polo (*seeing the audience*) Oooo! (*He comes forward and waves cheerfully to the audience*) Hallo!

"Hallo" from the audience

Rolo (*rushing to Polo, alarmed*) Hey! What do you think you're doing? We don't know who they are! They might not be very nice to know.
Polo I'll find out. (*To the audience*) *Are* you very nice to know?

"Yes" from the audience

(*To Rolo*) They're very nice to know. (*Pointing someone out*) Especially *that* one! Go on. Say "Hallo".
Rolo Well ... er ... we haven't been properly introduced.
Polo (*to the audience*) You'll have to forgive him. He once had a paper round at (*local posh area*)! This is my friend Rolo. Say hallo, Rolo.
Rolo (*to the audience, very formally*) How d' you do.
Polo Well, don't overdo it! (*To the audience*) There's not many about like Rolo. He's the *last* Rolo, in fact! (*He finds this highly amusing*)

Rolo doesn't

Rolo (*to the audience*) And this is Polo.

Polo bows low to the audience, then bows US

The one with the hole in the middle. But we won't go into that.
Polo (*straightening up and facing front*) I should hope not, indeed! (*To the audience*) I bet you can't guess what we are?

There is by-play and ad-libbing with the audience: "Don't be cheeky! You can go home!" etc., etc.

They haven't guessed, have they?
Rolo No. I suppose we'd better reveal our identities.
Polo You can get arrested for that!
Rolo (*to the audience*) We are servants to Septica. Septica, the Sorceress.
Polo The *evil* Sorceress! Have you heard of her?

"No" from the audience

You're lucky!
Rolo She's not a very nice person to work for.
Polo Nice! She makes (*current nasty*) look like Mary Poppins!

Rolo We should never have applied for the job. But we were desperate.
Polo Yeah! It was either work for her, or move to (*local place*)!
Rolo She's really horrible, and her temper is absolutely foul.
Polo (*grimacing*) Yeah! Especially at the moment!
Rolo Oh, yes. At the moment she's in a worse mood than usual because her favourite pair of magic shoes are at the Elf Cobbler's being repaired.
Polo And her spare pair are driving her mad! They're crippling her!
Rolo They're so uncomfortable, they've given her enormous bunions!
Polo And whackin' great blisters!
Rolo She's in agony!
Polo The best place for her!

They derive great pleasure from this, and chuckle together

Unseen by them, Septica, the Sorceress, enters L. Because of her uncomfortable shoes, she walks with a painful limp. She moves to behind the duo

The audience shouts warnings

The Demons emerge from behind the trees, and skulk in the background

Polo (*to the audience, with bravado*) Mind you, I'm not scared of her!
Rolo Nor me! Not a bit. Even though she's thoroughly evil.
Polo And nasty!
Rolo And utterly repulsive!
Polo And scary!
Rolo And ... (*sensing a presence, and gulping*) she's behind us, isn't she?!

Septica steps between the duo with a snarl; they cower away from her

Septica You dithering dolts! What are you doing? Why are you loitering here? Who are you talking to?

The duo points to the audience. Septica peers out at them, then snarls

So! You have been wasting my slaves' time, have you! Beware, you puny parasites! I am Septica, the Sorceress! The Queen of Sorcery! If you interfere in my plans, I will turn you all into crawling worms! *Oh, yes, I will!* (*She involves the audience in "Oh yes I will", "Oh no you*

won't" etc. When the routine has run its course) Enough! *(To the duo)*
Well! Where is he?
Duo W — Who?
Septica *(advancing on them)* Who? *Who?* Who do you think, you fools?
The Elf Cobbler, of course!
Rolo We haven't been able to find his tree yet, your evilness.
Polo No, your horribleness. They all look the same to us. We can't see
the tree for the wood!
Septica *(enraged)* You pathetic pair! *(She points to the tree* R*)* It's *that*
one! Get him out! *(She limps away* L *and nurses her sore feet)*

Rolo and Polo go to the tree R, *and search in vain for the door*

Rolo *(timidly)* Er ... We can't seem to find the door, your vileness.
Septica Knock! Knock!
Polo *(brightly)* Who's there?
Septica *(snarling)* You witless fools! Knock on the trunk!
Polo *(to Rolo)* You heard! Trock on the nunk ... Er ... Bang on the bark ...
Er ... Tap on the timber! Oh, just thump on the stump!

Rolo taps on the tree trunk

*The hitherto invisible door opens, and the Elf Cobbler sticks his head
out*

Elf Cobbler Sorry. It's early closing. Come back tomorrow! *(He makes
to disappear inside again)*
Septica *Seize him! Bring him before me!*

The duo obey and drag the Elf Cobbler over to Septica

Elf Cobbler *(nervously)* I ... I'm sorry about that. I didn't realize it was
you. A lovely morning for the time of year.
Rolo Very clement.
Polo I thought it was a bit nippy myself.
Septica *(enraged)* Silence!! Cobbler! Where are my shoes?
Elf Cobbler Your shoes ... Er ... Yes ... I'm afraid they're not quite ready
yet.
Septica *(advancing on the Elf, enraged)* Not ready! Not ready! You have
had two whole days to repair them! Two days in which I have had to
endure the agony of *these!* *(She points to her shoes)* They are killing
me! Crippling me! Each step I take is total torture! I want my comfy
shoes! I want them – *now!* *(To emphasize this, she stamps her foot. Of
course this causes her great pain, and she hops about in agony)*

Polo finds this amusing, until Rolo warns him

(*Roaring at the Elf*) I want my shoes!

Elf Cobbler And you shall have them. Give me another half an hour. I'm just putting the finishing touches to them.

Septica I will give you *ten minutes!* And if they are not ready in ten minutes, *I* will be putting the finishing touches to *you!* (*Snarling at him*) Now — *get on with it!*

The Elf Cobbler scuttles back into his tree, and shuts the door

(*Hobbling up and down, in pain*) Ooh! My feet! My poor feet! (*Snarling at the audience*) I suppose you enjoy seeing me suffer like this, don't you?

"Yes!" from the audience

Well, take care, or the boot will be on the other foot!

Polo (*laughing*) Ha! Ha! Ha! That's a good one! Boot on the other foot! Ha! Ha! Ha!

Septica advances threateningly towards Polo. His laughter dies. Polo and Rolo retreat DR

Septica I will not wait here in the presence of these (*indicating the audience*) mindless morons! Come! We shall return in ten minutes!

Septica limps out L, *snarling and sneering at the audience. The duo follow her out, with Polo doing a comic copy of her limp. The Demons exit behind the trees*

Molly (*off* UR; *calling*) Goody? ... Where are ya? .... Goody?

Molly Coddle creeps on UR. *She is closely followed by her son, Teddy. Both are very nervous of their surroundings. Molly creeps* DS *with Teddy keeping right up close behind her. They cross the stage in this fashion a couple of times, then come to a halt*

Molly (*calling in a frightened whisper*) Goody? ... Are you here, Goody? ... Goody?

Teddy (*bellowing*) *Goody!*

Molly (*yelling with fright*) Yaaaah! (*Rounding on Teddy*) What d'you think you're playin' at, Teddy Coddle? Ooh! You frightened me to death! Me whole life flashed before me! All twenty-one years of it!

Teddy It's no good whispering like that, Mum. Goody and the others won't hear you. You've got to (*bellowing in her ear*) *shout really loudly!*

Molly reacts, and rounds on Teddy

Molly Will you stop doin' that! I shall end up with percolated eardrums!

Teddy But we've got to let 'em know where we are, Mum. We're lost as well.

Molly I know that, Mastermind! And whose fault is it? Yours! (*Looking about her, scared*) Ooh! I've never been this deep into the forest before! It's all spooky an' creepy! Look at all those weird trees and plants! It's like Alan Titchmarsh's worst nightmare! It really gives me the jimjams ! Who knows what fearsome fiends frolic in this foul and forbidding foliage!

Teddy You can say that again, Mum.

Molly No, I can't — not with these teeth!

Teddy Don't be scared. You know the old saying — it's always darkest before you hide your light under a bushel. And don't forget, Mum — (*adopting a brave stance*) *I'm* with you!

Molly I know. That's part of the problem. (*She moves away from him*)

A mischievous grin spreads over Teddy's face. He is going to have some fun at her expense. Pretending to be very scared, he suddenly points L

Teddy What's that?

Molly (*rushing across to Teddy and clinging to him in fear*) What's what?

Teddy Nothing.

Molly (*relaxing*) Phew! (*She moves away from him*)

Teddy (*suddenly pointing to* R, *as before*) What's that?

Molly (*rushing back to Teddy and clinging to him*) What's what?

Teddy Nothing.

Molly Teddy Coddle! Are you tryin' to put the wind up me?

Teddy There's no need, Mum. You had baked beans for breakfast. (*He laughs*)

Molly (*pushing him*) Don't be coarse an' common! Be'ave yerself! (*She turns her back on him*)

Teddy turns away, smirking to himself. He sees the audience and is genuinely scared this time

Teddy (*pointing to the audience*) What's that? (*He just gapes at them, open-mouthed*)

Molly Oh, no! You don't catch me again. (*Turning*) I've 'ad enough of your … (*Reacting, and moving to him*) Teddy? What's the matter with ya? (*She waves her hand in front of his face, then looks him up and down*) Is it yer old trouble again? Teddy Coddle! Look at me when I'm talkin'! (*She turns his gaping face towards her*) Crickey! I can see what you 'ad for breakfast! (*Shaking him*) What's up with ya?

Teddy, zombie-like, raises his arm and points to the audience. Molly looks, does a huge double take, and leaps back with a yell. This brings Teddy back to life

Molly Yaaagh! (*Clinging to Teddy, and peering out at the audience*) It's a plot of leeple! Are they alive?

Teddy (*peering out*) I — I don't know … It's hard to tell … (*To the audience, timidly*) Are you alive?

A few replies from the audience

Molly They don't seem very sure, do they? (*Yelling at the audience*) *Are you alive?*

The audience yells back. Molly and Teddy react

Molly (*to Teddy, indicating the audience*) I told you there was some weird lookin' things in this forest!

Teddy They look all right to me.

Molly Yes, but you thought (*local gag*) was all right, didn't you? I suppose we'd better tell 'em who we are. (*To the audience*) I'm Molly Coddle. A poor widow. (*She encourages the audience to sigh*) No, I'm much poorer than that!

Teddy And I'm Teddy. Her poor son.

Molly I've got a daughter as well. Her name's Goody. You haven't seen her, 'ave ya? Oh, she's a lovely girl. She takes after me. (*Preening herself*) When I was 'er age I used to turn all the men's 'eads.

Teddy To say nothing of their stomachs!

Molly Watch it, you! We came into the forest with Goody and the Villagers to collect firewood. We should 'ave stuck with 'em, but Wonder Boy 'ere decided to wander off playin' at "I'm a celebrity! Get me out of 'ere"!

Teddy I didn't! I had to go for a ——

Molly (*clamping her hand over his mouth*) You needn't tell 'em your every movement! (*She removes her hand*) Ugh! (*She wipes her hand on Teddy. To the audience*) So now we're completely lost in this creepy, spooky old forest! Ooow! What are we gonna do? (*Clinging to Teddy and wailing*) I'm scared! I'm putrefied!

Teddy D'you know what I do when I get scared, Mum?

Molly Yes! And it's very embarrassin' at your age!

Teddy No, not that! I sing!

Song 2

A comedy song and dance for Teddy and Molly

If desired, the Demons can enter and participate in the background, unseen by Molly and Teddy. If used, they exit after the number

Teddy Feelin' better now, Mum?

Molly (*coughing and wheezing after the song*) Better than *what?* Oooh! I think I've lassoed me larynx!

Teddy Let's try looking for Goody and the others that way. (*Indicating* L) It doesn't look so dense.

Molly (*looking at him; pointedly*) It looks pretty dense from where I'm standin'! Go on then! Anything's better than 'angin' about 'ere, waitin' for somethin' nasty to pounce on us. Lead on, McDonalds!

Teddy takes Molly's hand, and leads her to the exit L

(*To the audience*) And if I don't see you again, it's been nice knowin' you.

Teddy Yes. You know the old saying: with friends like you who needs enemas! (*Waving*) Bye!

They exit

The door in the tree opens, and the Elf Cobbler emerges. He is holding a pair of glittering shoes

Elf Cobbler (*as he comes out*) Here are your shoes. All finished in under ten minutes. I ... Oh! (*Looking about*) She's not here! Phew! Thank goodness for that. (*Coming forward to speak to the audience confidentially*) I can't stand that horrible Sorceress. She's so ... Ugh! (*He grimaces and shivers*) Well, you've seen her, haven't you? I wish she'd take her magic shoes somewhere else to be repaired. Mind you, I *am* the finest cobbler in the whole of Elfdom. (*Holding up the shoes* *and admiring them)* Just look at that! Such skill! Such workmanship! You wouldn't know they had ever been repaired. I can't help doing splendid work, even for an awful old dragon like Septica. I put my heart and *soul* into it, you see. (*He chuckles*) Get it? Sole! (*He shows the soles of the shoes*) That's a cobbler's little joke, that is. And if you don't laugh, I shall feel a right *heel*. (*He hoots with laughter, then suddenly remembers the situation*) But I mustn't hang about here. I don't want to meet Septica again. (*Going up to his tree*) I'll just leave her shoes outside my tree. With any luck she'll take them away without bothering me. (*He puts the shoes on the ground in front of the tree, then steps into his doorway*) To see *her* twice in one day is enough to make Gandalf turn green! And that *isn't a* load of old cobblers! Cheerio!

With a quick wave, the Elf Cobbler disappears into his tree and shuts the door

Lively music is heard. With merry laughter, the Villagers dance on. In their midst is pretty young Goody Coddle

Song 3

Song and dance for Goody and Chorus

1st Villager We might be lost in the forest, but we're never lost for a song. Eh, Goody?
Goody That's true. I hope we find Mum and Teddy soon. This is certainly the spookiest place I've ever been in.

They all look at their creepy surroundings, and agree

2nd Villager It's even creepier than the (*local nightspot*)!
Goody It's not so bad for us, we're all together. But the thought of them alone and frightened in this place ...
3rd Villager Now don't worry, Goody. We'll find 'em soon.

A loud, despairing wail echoes from off L. *Goody and the others react with fright and huddle together*

1st Villager Oow! I — I don't like the sound of that!

The wail is repeated, coming nearer

3rd Villager (*terrified, pointing* L) Look! S—Something is coming this w—way!

They all retreat R

Molly blunders on L, *wailing and moaning. She is covered in greenery which obscures her head and face*

The others react in horror

Molly (*wailing*) Oooow!
1st Villager W — What is it?
2nd Villager It's a wild wisteria!
3rd Villager It's a furious fuchsia!
Molly (*wailing*) Oooow!!
Goody It's Mum!

Goody and the others rush across to Molly

Goody It's all right, Mum. It's us. We're here.

Goody and the Villagers remove the greenery from Molly's head and face

Molly Ooh! Goody! (*She hugs Goody*) Thank goodness! I've been in a right ... Hold on a minute! (*She taps the side of her head as if to dislodge something from her ear*) I think a squirrel left one of its nuts in me ear'ole! That's better. Ooh! Am I glad to see civilization again. (*To the others*) Even if it's only you lot! (*To the audience*) And you! (*Waving to them*) 'Allo, again! (*To someone in the front row*) Excuse the greenfly, luv!
Goody Mum ... Where's Teddy?
Molly Eh? (*Looking about*) You mean 'e isn't 'ere?!
Goody We haven't seen him.
Molly (*panicking*) Oh, no! What am I gonna do? My only son — *varnished without trace!*
1st Villager He can't be far away. Why don't you take us to the place where you last saw him?
Goody That sounds like a good idea, Mum.
Molly So does a night out with (*current male sex symbol*)! But I don't know where the place is! Teddy and me got completely lost, y'see. And then I got covered in Charlie Dimmock's cast offs! (*She performs comic business with the greenery*)

2nd Villager (*pointing* L) You came from over there. Let's try looking
for him in that direction.

Goody Right. You go with them, Mum. I'll wait here in case he comes
back this way.

Molly Oh, no! You're not stayin' 'ere on yer tod! Alone and
unprojected!

Goody I shall be all right, Mum.

Molly I'll make sure you are! I've 'ad an idea! Come with me. (*Leading
Goody forward; to the audience*) This is Goody. The daughter I was
tellin' you about. Say 'allo, Goody. They won't bite. (*Aside to her*)
Most of 'em have left their teeth at 'ome.

Goody (*waving to the audience*) Hallo, everybody.

"Hallos" from the audience

Molly (*to the audience*) Now, I want you to do me a big favour. While
we're off lookin' for Teddy, I want you to keep an eye on Goody for
me. Will you do that?

"Yes" from the audience

(*To a man in the audience*) And not *that* sort of eye, you mucky pup!
(*To all*) Tch! They'll let anyone in these days! I want you to make sure
nothin' nasty 'appens to her. Can I rely on you to do that?

"Yes" from the audience

Great! Thanks! (*To Goody*) Say thank you, Goody.

Goody Thank you, Goody!

Molly (*to the audience*) See! That's what you get for sendin' 'em to
(*local school/college*)! Right! I'll leave her in your hands. (*To the
man, archly*) And I don't mean that liberally! (*She kisses Goody*) Bye,
luvvie! We'll be back as soon as we've found that brother of yours.
(*Moving to the Villagers*) Come on, you lot! Into the dark inferior!

Molly and the Villagers move towards the exit L. *Molly stops*

(*Addressing the man in the audience*) And don't forget! I'm watchin'
you!

Molly and the Villagers exit L

Goody (*to the audience*) It's very kind of you to look after me, but there's really no need. I know this place is rather scary, but I don't think there's anything here that would harm me. Do you?

The Demons emerge from behind the trees and creep up behind Goody

The audience starts shouting warnings to her

Is there something here? Where is it?

"Behind you!" from the audience. The Demons hover right behind her

Behind me? Are you sure? Well, if you're that sure, I'd better take a look. (*She turns and sees the Demons*)

The Demons wave their arms at her, and make ghoulish noises. Goody is a little surprised, but shows no fear at all

(*To the Demons, as if talking to a stray kitten*) Hallo ... Hallo ... Where did you come from?

The Demons look at each other, with puzzled grunts. They then wave their arms even more fiercely and make even louder ghoulish noises. This still doesn't have the desired affect of frightening Goody

Goody (*smiling*) There's no need to be frightened. I'm not going to hurt you.

The Demons shrug. Deciding to give it up as a bad job, they amble away

(*Waving to them*) Goodbye ... Goodbye.

The Demons turn and give her a look, then disappear among the trees

Goody (*to the audience*) Poor things. It can't be much fun looking like leftovers from (*topical or local event*). (*She wanders over near to the Elf's tree*) I hope they find Teddy soon. He'll be ... (*She notices the shoes*) What's that? (*Moving closer*) It's a pair of shoes! (*She picks them up and admires them*) Oh! Aren't they beautiful! I wonder what they're doing here? Who'd leave such a lovely pair of shoes in a forest? They are nice. And they look to be my size too. I wonder ... Do you think it'd be all right if I tried them on?

"No!" from the audience

But what harm can it do? It's just a pair of shoes. I'm sorry, but I'm going to try them on. I just can't resist it! (*She quickly slips off her own shoes, and puts the others on*) Oh! They're so comfortable. (*She walks about, admiring the shoes*) You'd think they were made for me. And they look so wonderful! So elegant! I've never seen anything like them in (*local shoe shop*). They make me feel like dancing! (*She does a few dance steps*) They do look nice on me, don't they? (*Dreamily*) Oh, I *wish* there was someone really special to see me wearing them. Someone who would instantly fall in love with me. (*She sighs, then goes back to admiring the shoes*)

A magical effect takes place, unnoticed by Goody. There is a lighting change and magical sounds are heard. (See Production Notes)

Simon, a handsome young man, enters DL, unseen by Goody. He sees Goody and stands watching her at a distance

The lighting returns to normal and the magical sounds fade

Goody (*sadly*) Oh, well! I suppose I'd better take them off. After all, they don't belong to me. (*She attempts to remove a shoe, balancing on one leg*)
Simon (*crossing to Goody*) Can I help?

His sudden appearance causes Goody to lose her balance and she starts to topple

Goody Oh!
Simon (*catching her in his arms*) Steady!

There is a pause while they gaze into each other's eyes. It is obviously love at first sight!

Goody (*still in his arms*) I ... I'm all right now ... Thank you ... You can let go of me.
Simon (*smiling*) Oh, that's a shame.

They part

What were you doing anyway?
Goody I was trying to take off these shoes.

Simon What on earth for? (*Looking at the shoes*) They're very nice-looking shoes. (*His eyes travel up to her face*) Very nice-looking indeed.

Goody (*embarrassed*) I ... I know they are. But they're not mine, you see. I found them. They were ... (*Suddenly alarmed*) Oh, dear! They're not *yours*, are they?

Simon (*laughing*) Hardly! Do they look like something I'd wear?

Goody Well, they could belong to your sister — or girlfriend.

Simon As I'm not blessed with either, the answer to that is no. Besides, they look very expensive. Well out of my league. My name is Simon, by the way. (*He holds out his hand*)

Goody (*shaking his hand*) Goody.

Simon (*still holding her hand*) I'm so glad you're pleased.

Goody (*laughing*) No, that's my name. Goody. Goody Coddle.

Simon And what are you doing alone in this forest, Goody Coddle?

Goody Oh, I'm not alone.

Simon (*releasing her hand*) Ah! I suppose there's a boyfriend lurking behind one of those trees.

Goody Oh, no. I mean I'm here with my family and some of the villagers. They've gone looking for my brother Teddy. We've lost him.

Simon And they've left you here on your own?

Goody Not exactly. (*She points out to the audience*) My friends have been looking after me. (*To the audience*) Haven't you?

"Yes" from the audience

Simon (*to the audience, giving the "thumbs up"*) Well done! (*To her*) Perhaps you'll let *me* look after you as well, Goody. (*He takes her hand*)

Goody Yes ... I'd like that, Simon.

Song 4

A romantic duet and dance with romantic lighting. It ends with Goody and Simon in an embrace

Molly, now without the greenery, and Teddy rush on L. *They are followed by the Villagers*

Molly We've found 'im! We've ... (*She pulls up short at the sight of the embracing couple*) Oy! Oy! Oy! (*Rushing across and pushing them apart*) What's goin' on 'ere? Who are you? What are you doing to our Goody? (*To the man in the audience*) And I was worried about *you*!

(*To Simon*) Come on! Come on! I'm waitin' for you to give me a full exploration!

Goody It's all right, Mum. This is Simon.

Molly I don't care if it's Simon and Carbuncle! How dare you take advantage of my daughter! How double dare you! Teddy Coddle! You're 'er brother! Are you just gonna stand there!

Teddy (*doing just that*) Yes, Mum. Where else do you want me to stand?

Simon (*to Molly*) Please let me elucidate.

Molly I think you've done enough of that, young man!

Goody Mum, listen. Simon wasn't doing anything I didn't *want* him to do.

Molly (*shocked*) Y — You mean — you *let* 'im! (*O.T.T., tragic*) Oh! My only daughter — *a scallop!*

Simon Mrs Coddle, let me explain. Goody and I love each other.

Molly *Love?* Is this true, Goody? Do you love this reject from (*something appropriate to Simon's costume*)?

Goody I do. With all my heart!

Goody and Simon embrace. Teddy "Ahhs!" and encourages the audience to join in

Molly All right! All right! A simple "yes" would 'ave done! (*Coming forward to speak to the audience*) I dunno! Kids these days! They fall in love at the drop of a hat, don't they? (*To someone*) It was different in our day, wasn't it, dear? You 'ad to know a man for three years before you'd drop yer *guard,* never mind yer *'at!* (*She goes back to Goody and Simon, who are still embracing*) Break!! You can come up for air now!

They part

Well, if you really do love each other I suppose it's all right by me.

Goody (*hugging Molly*) Thank you, Mum!

Simon Thank you, Mrs Coddle.

Molly Call me Molly.

Simon hugs Molly. Teddy and the others gather around to congratulate the couple

Teddy (*to Goody*) Nice one, Goody! (*To Simon*) I'd like to offer you my felicitations. But I don't know where I put 'em! Ha! Ha! Ha! (*He guffaws at his "joke"*)

Molly (*to Simon*) You'll 'ave to excuse 'im. 'Is father spent a lot of time in (*local place*)!

Teddy (*noticing Goody's shoes for the first time*) Hey, sis! Where did you get the fancy footwear?

Goody displays the shoes to Molly and the others

The door in the tree opens a fraction, and the Elf Cobbler peeps out to watch and listen, unseen by everyone onstage

Molly Ooh! They're real bobby-dazzlers, aren't they? Must 'ave cost a bomb! (*To Simon*) Did you buy 'er those? I'm likin' you more by the minute, young man.

Goody I found them.

Teddy Found them?

Goody Yes. They were just lying under a tree. I couldn't resist trying them on.

1st Villager What are you going to do with them, Goody?

Goody Put them back where I found them, I suppose.

Molly Put 'em back! Put 'em back! Don't talk so giddy, Goody!

Teddy No. You know the old saying — finders keepers, and never look a gift horse in the mouth after you've bolted the stable door!

Molly (*to him*) Shurrup! (*To Goody*) You keep 'em, luv!

Goody But suppose the owner comes looking for them?

Molly They can't care much about 'em. They wouldn't leave 'em lying around if they did.

Goody (*unsure*) Oh, I don't know ... What do *you* think I should do, Simon?

Simon Well, they did bring us together in a manner of speaking — I think you should keep them.

Goody Very well. I will.

Elf Cobbler (*groaning audibly*) Oh, no!

Realizing he might have been heard, the Elf Cobbler quickly disappears back into his tree and shuts the door

Teddy *What's that?*

Molly (*to him, threateningly*) Don't start that again!

Teddy No, I definitely 'eard somethin'! It was a sort of — *groaning!*

Molly Oh, you're imaginin' things! You're gettin' Polaroid! Let's go 'ome!

Teddy D'you think that's a good idea, Mum? What about the new landlord?

Molly (*alarmed*) Oh, crikey! I forgot about 'im! 'E's comin' to collect 'is rent today!

Goody And?

Molly Well, I — I 'aven't got it.

Goody What do you mean?

Molly I 'aven't 'ad it for years!

Teddy There's no answer to that! (*He giggles*)

Molly Shurrup, you! (*To Goody*) Y' see, I never paid any rent to the old landlord. He and I had a — er — a sort of arrangement. I used to give him a hand with 'is smallholding sometimes. Anyway, last week 'e sold our cottage to some stranger called Titus Tightwad. I don't know who 'e is, but *'e's* our landlord now.

Simon (*showing concern*) Did you say Titus Tightwad?

Molly With some difficulty, yes.

Simon Oh, dear!

Goody Do you know him, Simon?

Simon Only by reputation. I'm afraid I have to tell you that Titus Tightwad is a money-grabbing old miser! Only last week he evicted a family in our village for missing one rent payment.

Molly (*groaning*) Oh! That's it then! There's nothin' else for it! Teddy!

Teddy Yes, Mum?

Molly Go and reserve us a nice dry place in the gutter! (*She starts crying*)

Goody (*going to comfort her*) Don't upset yourself, Mum.

Molly But 'e'll want 'is rent! And I can't pay it! To say nothin' of all the back rent that's owin'! Oh! What are we gonna do?

Teddy I know! We'll hide from him!

Molly You stupid boy!

Teddy No, listen. If he can't find us, he can't ask us for the rent, can he? You know the old saying: out of sight, out of the frying pan.

Molly (*warming to the idea*) You're right, Teddy! Yes! That's what we'll do! We'll hide from old Tightwad! I've 'ad plenty of experience at 'idin' from graspin' men in my time! (*To the others*) Come on! Let's try and find our way out of this flippin' forest.

Simon I think the way out lies in that direction. (*He indicates* UR)

Molly If you get us out of 'ere in one piece, young Simon, and you can come to lunch.

Simon (*pleased*) Thank you very much indeed.

Molly Oh, don't thank me! You 'aven't seen Teddy's eatin' habits yet! Lead on!

Led by Simon and Goody, they all exit UR, *Teddy and Molly waving goodbye to the audience as they go*

A slight pause

The door in the tree opens slowly, and the Elf Cobbler peeps out. Seeing the coast is clear, he emerges. He picks up Goody's old shoes from beside the tree, then does a frantic search about the stage for the magic pair. Finally, he gives a sigh of despair and turns to the audience

Elf Cobbler That young girl took the magic shoes away with her, didn't she?

"Yes" from the audience

(*Pacing up and down in great agitation*) Oh, dear! Oh, dear! Oh, dear! (*He stops pacing*) You know what this means, don't you? That horrible Septica is going to blame *me!* She'll say it was *my* fault! Who knows what awful things she'll do to me! Oh! I should never have left them outside! (*He paces again*) Oh, dear! Oh, dear! Oh, dear! (*He stops pacing*) What am I going to do? She'll be back at any moment! (*He paces again*) What shall I do? What shall I do? (*He stops pacing*) I know! I'll run away! *That's* what I'll do!

Still clutching Goody's shoes, he runs to the exit DR

Rolo and Polo enter DR

The Elf Cobbler pulls up short. He runs across to the exit DL

Septica limps on DL

The Elf Cobbler runs US

The Demons emerge US *and block his escape*

Terrified, the Elf Cobbler turns and retreats DS. *Septica and the duo close in on him*

Septica (*sneering at the audience*) Pah! I see those puny little parasites are still here!

By-play with the audience

(*Turning to the Elf Cobbler*) I have returned for my precious pair of shoes! I have been more than generous, and given you far longer than ten minutes. So! They had better be ready! Ah! I see you have them there! Give them to me!

Elf Cobbler B-But these aren't your ——
Septica (*snarling at him*) Don't keep me waiting any longer! *Give me those shoes!*

The Elf Cobbler tremulously gives her Goody's old shoes. He then shrinks back, preparing for the worst

At last! My precious shoes! My ... (*She becomes aware of what she is holding, and lets out an ear-splitting scream of rage*) AHHHHHHHGH!! Seize that Elf!

Rolo and Polo take hold of the trembling Elf Cobbler, Rolo on his R, Polo on his L. Septica limps across and towers over him, seething with rage

What have you done to them? What have you done to my lovely shoes? *Look at them!* (*She thrusts them under his nose*) You've destroyed them! You've turned them into something hideous! They now look like the sort of shoes *they* (*pointing to the audience*) would wear! Cobbler, you will pay dearly for this! I'll ——
Elf Cobbler (*trembling*) T —Those aren't your shoes!
Septica What?
Elf Cobbler They belong to the young girl who ... (*gulping*) who ...
Septica Who *what?*
Elf Cobbler (*blurting it out*) Who took yours.
Septica (*in disbelief*) Took mine? What are you saying? Have my shoes been — *stolen?*
Elf Cobbler Well ... Er ... Sort of.
Septica (*letting out another ear-splitting scream of rage*) AHHHHHHHGH!!!

Septica stamps her feet, in her rage. This causes her pain, and she hops about in agony. Rolo and Polo are hard put to suppress their delight and laughter. Septica regains control of herself

(*Snarling at the cringing Elf Cobbler*) Who is she? Who is this wretched girl that has dared to steal *my* shoes? Tell me who she is, or I will have you — *roasted alive!*
Rolo (*to the Elf Cobbler*) She means it!
Polo Yeah! She's just bought a brand new barbecue from (*local store*)!
Elf Cobbler (*pleading to Septica*) I swear I don't know! All I know is — they called her — Goody.
Septica (*with disgust*) Goody! *Goody!* Ugh! What a repulsive name! And where does she live, this Goody? Tell me where I can find her!
Elf Cobbler I — I don't know!

Septica Very well! (*To the duo*) Take this worm away! (*With evil relish*) *And start heating the charcoal!*
Polo At once, your viciousness! (*He snaps to attention, stamping his feet and saluting. Accidentally (on purpose!) he manages to stamp on Septica's foot*)

Septica yells in agony and hops away US. While she is thus occupied, Rolo and Polo release the Elf Cobbler, and push him toward the front of the stage

Rolo (*aside to the Elf Cobbler*) Now's your chance!
Polo (*ditto*) Run for it!

The Elf Cobbler runs off the stage and down into the auditorium. He hides among the audience. Rolo and Polo watch his progress from the front of the stage. Fuming with rage, Septica hobbles down to them

Septica You fools! You imbeciles! You've let him escape! Don't just stand there! Get after him! *Find him!!*

Rolo and Polo go down into the auditorium. Comic business ensues as they pretend to search among the audience for the Elf Cobbler, with ad libs, i.e. "Here he is! Oh, no! It's only a Mrs So and So!" etc., etc.

Eventually Rolo and Polo smuggle the Elf Cobbler out through the back exit of the auditorium. This done, they make their way back to the stage

Rolo I'm afraid he's eluded us, your evilness!
Polo Yeah! And he's bun a dunk! ... Er ... Dunked a bun! ... Er ... Oh, he's run away!
Septica He can't get far. Later I shall seek him out and deal with him! At the moment there is a more urgent matter to attend to. My precious shoes must be found and returned to me! Along with the wretch who has stolen them! This Goody person will be severely punished for taking what belongs to me! (*Turning on the duo*) You two! Go to the village that lies beyond the forest. I have no doubt she dwells there. Seek her out! There cannot be many with such a ridiculous name as Goody! You will return within the hour with my shoes and the thief!

The duo shows some apprehension

(*Advancing on them, threateningly*) Be warned! If I am forced to come looking for you — in these *very* uncomfortable shoes — you know what will happen — (*snarling at them*) *don't you?*

Rolo }
Polo } (*cringing away*) Oh, yes!
Septica Then do not fail me! Go!

Rolo and Polo rush out DR, *falling over themselves*

Septica (*to the audience*) When I have finished with this wretched Goody, she will wish she had never set eyes on my magic shoes, let alone steal them! (*With evil relish*) Oh, I will make her suffer! Oh, yes, I will!

A routine with the audience ensues. Finally, Septica stamps her foot to emphasis her point. This causes her great pain

Septica hobbles out DL, *snarling and shaking her fist at the audience*

The Demons come forward, and go into a short reprise of their song and dance

Reprise Song 1

The number ends with a tableau

The Lights fade to Black-out

Music is played to cover the scene change

SCENE 2

Near the village

Tabs, or a frontcloth showing a country road with the village in the distance

The Lights come up

A few of the Villagers stroll on DL. *They pause* C *to chat among themselves*

Tightwad (*loud, disgruntled, off* DR) Baah! Where is the confounded woman!

The Villagers, hearing this, look towards the DR *exit*

1st Villager Who on earth is that?
2nd Villager I don't know, but he doesn't look very happy.
3rd Villager Hey! I wonder if it's that miserly old Titus Tightwad, Molly Coddle's new landlord.
2nd Villager Oh, yes! The one she's hiding from.
1st Villager Look out! He's coming this way! Now remember — we don't know where Molly is. Act dumb!

The Villagers adopt attitudes of dumb rustics

Titus Tightwad stomps on from DR, grumbling to himself. He looks exactly what he is, an old miser

Tightwad Bah! I'll find the wretched woman, if it's the last thing I do! (*Seeing the villagers*) Ah! Perhaps she's one of these clodhoppers! (*Crossing to them, and addressing one of the women*) Are you Molly Coddle?
1st Woman (*playing the dumb rustic*) Eh?
Tightwad (*impatiently*) I said — are you Molly Coddle?
Woman Not when there be a R in the month, zur.
Tightwad Oh, never mind! (*To another woman*) Are *you* Molly Coddle?
2nd Woman Eh?
Tightwad Bah! I am looking for a woman!
Man (*winking and nudging Tightwad*) Arr!! Bain't we all, zur.
Tightwad Her name is Molly Coddle. Do you know where she is?
2nd Woman It don't stop yere, zur.
Tightwad What?
2nd Woman The bus to (*local place*).
Man No, zur. It do only stop at Upper Sheep's Bottom!
2nd Woman An' this be *Lower* Sheep's bottom!
Man An' then it do only stop durin' muck spreadin'!
All Villagers (*nodding in agreement*) Oh, Arr!
Tightwad (*shaking his head in disbelief*) I think I've wandered into an episode of *The Archers*! (*To them, exasperated*) Oh, just — go away! *Go away!*
All Villagers Arr!

The Villagers exit DR, giggling

Tightwad (*to the audience*) I bought that cottage at a very low price. I got it for next to nothing, in fact. (*He gives a miserly cackle, then becomes disgruntled again*) And now I know why! Molly Coddle, the

sitting tenant, has not paid a penny in rent since she's been living there!
Not one brass farthing! By my calculations she owes *two hundred
pounds* in back rent! Well! I mean to get it from her! Oh, yes! Every
single penny! The trouble is, I can't find the wretched woman! I've
been to the cottage *six* times this morning, and she's not there! Bah!
And if that wasn't bad enough, I have Cissie staying with me! My
obnoxious niece! She's eating me out of house and home! I've had to
order an extra pint of milk a week because of her! I only put up with
her because one day she will inherit a fortune from her dead father.
A very sizable fortune! (*He cackles and rubs his hands together*) And
being her guardian, I hope to have the use of it! But I really can't stand
the spoilt brat!

Cissie (*calling, from off* DL) Uncle Tituth! Uncle Tituth!

Tightwad (*wincing*) Ugh! That sounds like her now! I'm off! (*He heads
towards the exit* DR)

Cissie enters from DL, *She is possibly in her late teens or early twenties,
but still behaves and dresses like a little girl. She believes this makes
her appear cute and adorable, which of course it doesn't! She also has
a very pronounced lisp*

Cissie Uncle Tituth! Uncle Tituth! (*She skips over to him and grabs his
arm*) I've been looking everywhere for you, you thilly old thauthage!
I want to ath you for thomthing.

Tightwad (*aside, to the audience*) See what I mean! (*To Cissie, eager to
be gone*) What is it, Cissie? Make it quick. I'm very busy.

Cissie I want ... (*She sees the audience*) Oooh! (*She releases Tightwad,
and moves down to peer at the audience. She views them with obvious
displeasure*) Ugh! What are all theath *common* perthonth doing here?
Ugh! They all look tho *nathty* and *thmelly!* Pooh! I can *thmell* them
from here! And look at their horrible clotheth! They look like nathty
old tharecrowth! (*Preening herself*) Not like me! (*Showing off her
dress*) My clotheth are much nither than yourth! Oh, yeth, they are!

*An "Oh, no, they're not!/"Oh, yeth, they are!" routine with the audience
follows. Finally, Cissie pokes her tongue out at them, and goes to
Tightwad*

They've been ever tho nathty to me, Uncle Tituth! Thend them away!

Tightwad I can't do that, Cissie. They've all paid to be here. (*To the
audience, scowling*) At least, I *hope* they have! (*To her*) Now, what is
it you want? I have to go and collect some money!

Cissie Tha'th juth want I want! Thome money.

Tightwad You mean you want *my* money?

Cissie Yeth pleath. I've juth theen thith thooper dooper new hat!

Tightwad A hat?

Cissie Yeth! Oh, it'th thimply thrumpthuth! I've got to have it!

Tightwad (*suspiciously*) How much is it?

Cissie It'th only fifty poundth.

Tightwad (*having a fit*) F... F... Fifty pounds! For a hat? What is it made of — gold? No! It's out of the question! (*He turns to go, grumbling to himself*) Pah! Fifty pounds for a hat! Ridiculous!

Cissie Uncle Tituth. If you don't give me the fifty poundth, I thall thcream an' thcream an' *thcream!*

Tightwad Bah! Do as you like! I'm got giving you a penny! (*He turns to go*)

True to her word, Cissie screams the place down. Tightwad just ignores her. Eventually, Cissie runs out of steam, and stands there panting

(*To the audience, unconcerned*) Did you hear something? (*He starts to go*)

Cissie Uncle Tituth?

Tightwad The answer is no!

Cissie (*playing the innocent*) I've been thinking. When I inherit my fortune, I might want thomeone elth to be my guardian, and not you.

Tightwad (*turning, on the alert*) What's that? What did you say? What do you mean?

Cissie But if you gave me the money to buy the new hat ...

Tightwad (*reluctantly giving in*) Oh, very well! You win! Bah! (*He goes to his pocket, then stops*) Turn away!

Cissie turns her back on him, very pleased with herself. Tightwad hauls a long chain with a small purse attached to the end of it from his pocket. He starts to open the purse, becomes aware of the audience, and turns his back on them with a "Bah!"

Tightwad (*from over his shoulder*) How much is it, did you say? Ten pounds?

Cissie Fifty!

Tightwad Bah! (*He rummages in the purse and produces the bank note, grumbling to himself. He looks at it lovingly, even kisses it goodbye, then holds it out to Cissie*) Here!

Cissie (*turning and snatching the note*) Oh! Thank you tho much, Uncle Tituth!

Tightwad Bah! (*He quickly stows away the chain and purse*)
Cissie (*looking at the note*) Oh, look! The Queen'th blinking in the thunlight! (*She giggles*)
Tightwad (*certainly not amused*) Very funny! Bah!

Tightwad stomps out DR, *grumbling to himself*

Cissie (*to the audience, with a contemptuous laugh*) Ha! Ha! Look! *I've* got fifty poundth! I bet *you* haven't! I bet *you* haven't even got fifty *penth!* 'Coth you're all tho *poor* and *thcruffy!* Not like me! I'm tho glamorouth! I make Barbie look like (*current "scruff"*)! And when I've bought my new hat, I thall look even more beautiful and cute! Oh, yeth, I will!

There is an "Oh, no, you won't!", "Oh, yeth, I will!" routine with the audience. It ends with Cissie poking her tongue out at them, and flouncing out DL

Molly creeps on cautiously DR. *As in the previous scene, Teddy follows very closely behind her. They move about the stage in this fashion, then Molly stops* C *and faces front. Teddy stays hidden behind her*

Molly (*looking to her* R) There's no one ... Teddy? (*Looking to her* L) Teddy? Where are ya? (*She looks right again*)
Teddy (*popping out right in front of her*) Here!
Molly (*jumping with fright*) Yaaaagh!! (*Rounding on Teddy*) You great soft nellie!
Teddy Sorry, Mummy.
Molly So you ought to be! Oh! You could 'ave given me cardigan arrest!
Teddy (*indicating the audience*) Hey! Look, Mum! Our mates are still here!
Molly So they are!
Both (*waving to the audience*) Hallo, folks!

"Hallos" from the audience

Molly We've 'eard old Tightwad is lookin' for me. 'Ave you seen 'im?

"Yes" from the audience

Teddy And is he a horrible grasping old miser?

"Yes" from the audience. Molly and Teddy react

Molly You're on our side, aren't you, folks?

"Yes" from the audience

Good! So, if 'e comes by, you'll let us know, won't ya?

"Yes" from the audience. Teddy and Molly give them the "thumbs up"

Cissie enters DL. *She is now wearing a large and ludicrous hat. It is decorated with lots of false fruit and flowers. She thinks it makes her look wonderful, of course*

Cissie parades up and down, showing off the hat. Molly and Teddy gaze at her in amazement, then burst out laughing

Cissie (*stomping up to them; indignantly*) Are you laughing at *me?*
Molly Well, I don't see anyone else wearin' a grow bag on their 'ead!

Molly and Teddy hoot with laughter. Pouting and upset, Cissie turns her back on them. Teddy notices this, and stops laughing. Molly's laughter subsides, and she holds her sides in pain

Molly Oooh! I'll 'ave to go 'ome! I think I've done meself a mischief! (*She staggers to the* DR *exit, clutching her sides. She turns to look at Cissie, and starts hooting with laughter again*)

Molly stumbles out DR

Teddy approaches Cissie

Teddy I ... I'm sorry about that.
Cissie Go away!
Teddy (*trying his best*) I quite like your hat really. You know the old saying: beauty is in the eye of the needle that broke the camel's back.
Cissie Go away!
Teddy My name's Teddy. Teddy Coddle. That was my mum, Molly Coddle.
Cissie Who careth! Go away! (*Turning and snarling at Teddy*) Go away!
Teddy (*reacting*) I ... I think I'll ... er ... go away.

Teddy makes an awkward exit DR

Cissie (*to the audience*) I don't care what they thay about my hat. I think it'th lovely! And *I'm* lovely too!

Song 5

Song and dance for Cissie and the Chorus (Note: If space is limited, this can be a solo number for Cissie)

Unseen by Cissie, some of the Villagers enter

The Villagers are amused at the sight of Cissie's hat. They join her in the song and dance. Cissie is blissfully unaware that they are just making fun of her. The number ends with a tableau, then the Villagers point to her hat and roar with laughter. In a rage, Cissie chases them DR

The Villagers exit DR

Cissie makes faces and pokes her tongue out after the Villagers, then applies the same treatment to the audience

Goody and Simon enter DL

They are too engrossed in each other to notice Cissie. But she notices them. At least, she notices Simon — and how!

Cissie Oooow! Who'th he? Ith'nt he handthome! Oooow! I really fanthee him! (*She adjusts her hat and preens herself, then crosses to the couple. She adopts what she thinks is her cutest and most endearing pose. In her best baby doll voice*) Hallo.

The couple turn. They are surprised to see such an apparition. To say nothing of the hat! Cissie only has eyes for Simon and completely ignores Goody

Simon Oh! ... Hallo.
Cissie (*batting her eyelashes at him*) I'm Thithie.
Simon I'm sorry to hear that.
Cissie (*giggling*) No! Thath my name, you thilly boy! Thithie! It'th thort for Thethelia.
Simon Oh, I thee ... er ... see. I'm pleased to meet you, Cissie. My name is Simon.
Cissie (*with a soppy wave*) Hallo, Thimon!
Simon And this is Goody.
Goody (*to Cissie*) How do you ——

But Cissie pushes past Goody so that she can be next to Simon. Goody is not offended by this and views Simon's forthcoming discomfort with amusement

Cissie (*playing up to Simon for all she is worth*) Do you like my hat, Thimon?
Simon Er ... Yes ... It's very — different.
Cissie It cotht fifty poundth!
Simon Really?
Cissie Yeth. Do you think I look nithe in it?
Simon Er ... Oh, yes!
Cissie I look jutht ath nithe without it.
Simon I'm sure you do.
Cissie (*coyly*) Thimon?
Simon Yes?
Cissie Will you be my thooter?
Simon Your scooter?
Cissie (*giggling*) Not a thooter, you thilly boy! *Thooter!* Ath in — boyfriend! (*She moves in very close to him and flutters her eyelashes*)
Simon Ah! Well ... You see ... I'm already somebody else's boyfriend.
Cissie (*indignantly*) Thomebody eltheth?
Simon Yes. (*He quickly moves to Goody and takes her by the hand*) Goody's.
Cissie (*aghast*) Herth? (*Looking at Goody with disgust*) Ugh! But the'th tho *poor* and *common!* Look at her dreary dreth! Ugh! Look at her horrid hair! Ugh! The'th a meth!
Simon (*offended for Goody*) There's no need to be rude!
Goody My clothes may be a little shabby, but I do have a very nice pair of shoes. (*She displays her shoes*)
Cissie (*looking at them with a snort of disgust*) Pah! They're horrid! I've got *lot'th* and *lot'th* of thoeth much nither than thothe! (*To Simon, whining*) Why would you rather be her boyfriend than *mine?*
Simon Because I love her.
Cissie (*starting to pout*) But I'm much prettier than her! (*To the audience*) I am, aren't I?

"No!" from the audience. An "Oh, yeth I am!/Oh, no, you're not!" routine with the audience follows

It ends with Cissie stomping out in a rage, making faces and poking her tongue out at the audience as she exits

Goody (*laughing*) Does this mean I have a rival?

Simon Well, that hat certainly puts you in the shade.

They both laugh

I'd like to go home before joining you for lunch.

Goody All right. That's our cottage over there. Although I'm not sure what's going to happen about lunch. What with Mum hiding from the new landlord.

Simon I don't care what happens as long as you're there.

Goody (*mimicking Cissie*) Oh, you *thilly* boy, you!

They laugh and embrace

Simon exits DL

Goody follows Simon to the exit and waves goodbye

Rolo and Polo creep on DR *unseen by Goody. They pull up short on seeing her and converse together in hushed tones*

Rolo Look! It's a girl!

Polo *There's no fooling you, is there!*

Rolo See what she's wearing?

Polo Is it —— (*the latest make-up/perfume as advertised on TV*)?

Rolo No! *The* shoes! She's wearing Septica's magic shoes!

Polo Yeah! You're right! She must be Goody. What are we gonna do?

Rolo Take her and the shoes back to Septica, of course. Come on. Let's grab her!

They creep up behind Goody

The audience will be shouting warnings

Goody (*to the audience*) What's wrong? Is there someone there? Where are they?

"Behind you!" from the audience

Behind me?

There follows business with Goody turning around and the duo always keeping behind her. Eventually, they come face to face. Goody shows no surprise or fear. Rolo and Polo show a lot of both. They are frozen and dumbstruck!

Goody (*greeting them with a warm smile*) Hallo. My name's Goody.
Can I help you?

No response

Are you looking for someone?

Again, no response

Is there somewhere you want to go?

No response

Well, if I can't be of any help, I'd best be on my way. Goodbye ...
Goodbye. (*She goes to the exit* DR, *stops to look back at the frozen
pair, then turns to the audience*) Poor things. I expect they're from
(*local place*).

Goody exits DR. *A pause. The duo remains frozen*

Polo (*out of the corner of his mouth*) I think she's gone.
Rolo (*coming back to life*) Of course she's gone, you nitwit! *You* let her
get away!
Polo Me? I like that! I notice you didn't do much to stop her! *Let's grab
her,* you said!
Rolo Well, when it came down to it — I didn't have the heart.
Polo Nor me. She's so sweet and pretty, isn't she?
Rolo And friendly too. We can't take a nice girl like her back to that
awful Sorceress.
Polo No way. But if we don't — old Septica will have our bums for
plate racks!
Rolo You know what this is called, don't you?
Polo A load of old rubbish?
Rolo A dilemma!
Polo (*wincing*) Ugh! I had that once! Very painful!
Rolo There must be some way out of this. Let's think!

They think for a while

Polo Hey! I've just had a thunk! What if we get the shoes — take them
back to Septica — and tell her we disposed of Goody while gettin'
'em!
Rolo Yes! Once she's got her precious shoes back, Septica will forget
all about it. That way Goody won't get hurt. A brilliant idea! (*Patting
Polo's head*) Well done.

Polo (*very pleased with himself*) See! I'm not just an ugly face!
Rolo We'd better get on with it. Time's running out.
Polo Yeah! We don't want old niggle knickers comin' after us!

They move to the exit, then stop

Rolo (*to the audience*) Aren't you going to wish us good luck?

"Good luck!" from the audience

Polo Oh, come on! We're gonna need more good luck than *that!*

More "Good luck!" calls from the audience

Waving goodbye, Rolo and Polo exit DR

The Lights fade to Black-out

Music is played to cover the scene change

SCENE 3

Outside Molly's cottage

Prominent L *is Molly's quaint, but tumbledown cottage. It has a practical front door. The backcloth and side wings show the rest of the village*

The Lights come up. The Villagers are discovered in a merry song and dance

Song 6

After the number, Tightwad stomps on R

Tightwad pushes through the Villagers on his way to the cottage, grumbling to himself. He hammers on the front door, then paces up and down, impatiently

The Villagers quickly confer, then adopt the attitudes of dumb rustics

Tightwad hammers on the door again, and paces up and down

Tightwad Bah! Still not in! Confound the wretched woman! (*Turning to the others*) Do any of you know where Molly Coddle is?

All Villagers (*with exaggerated dumbness*) Eh?

Tightwad (*exasperated*) Oh, no! Not again! (*To the audience*) I thought
they were stupid in (*local place*), but *this* lot really takes the biscuit!
(*To the others*) Go away!

All Villagers Arr!

They exit in various directions, giggling among themselves

Tightwad (*to the audience*) Bah! Molly Coddle will have to return to
the cottage sometime! And when she does — I will catch her! Oh,
yes, I will!

*There is an "Oh, no you won't", "Oh, yes I will" routine with the
audience, then Tightwad stomps off R*

A slight pause

Molly creeps on L. She looks cautiously about

Molly (*to the audience*) Hallo, folks! Is old Tightwad about?

"Yes" from the audience

'E is! Oh, dear! What am I gonna do? I know! I'll nip inside and
pretend I'm not at 'ome! (*To someone*) I bet *you've* done that as well,
'aven't you, dear? (*She goes to the cottage, then comes back*) Listen.
If 'e comes back, you 'aven't seen me. Right?

"Yes" from the audience

Great! Thanks, folks! I knew I could rely on you!

Tightwad enters from R, unseen by Molly

*Tightwad sees Molly, and slowly moves towards her. The audience will
be shouting warnings*

Eh? What's that? Is it 'im?

"Yes" from the audience

I'll 'ave to bluff me way out of this! Remember — I'm *not* Molly
Coddle!

Tightwad (*confronting her*) Ah!

Molly (*turning and reacting*) Ahhhgh!

Tightwad I'm Tightwad.

Molly Ooh! That sounds painful! (*Looking him up and down*) 'Ave you tried the next size up?

Tightwad Are you Molly Coddle?

Molly Colly Moddle?

Tightwad (*impatiently*) Molly Coddle! *Molly Coddle!*

Molly Oh, stop talkin' such twaddle! Off I waddle for a toddle. (*She starts to move off*)

Tightwad (*stopping her*) Just a minute! Answer me! (*Shouting at her*) *Are you Molly Coddle?*

Molly (*shouting back*) No, *I'm not!*

Tightwad Bah! I don't believe you! You're trying to bamboozle me.

Molly Huh! I never touched yer bam, or yer boozle!

Tightwad If you're *not* Molly Coddle, why are you loitering outside her cottage?

Molly *Loiterin'!* Listen, Mr Tightpants, or whatever yer name is, I can loit wherever I like to loit! If you don't believe *me* — ask *them!* (*To the audience*) I'm not Molly Coddle, am I?

"No!" from the audience

There!

Tightwad Hummph! (*To the audience, with suspicion*) Are you absolutely sure about that?

From behind Tightwad's back, Molly encourages them to answer "Yes"

Positive?

"Yes" from the audience

(*Grudgingly conceding to Molly*) Very well. It seems you are telling me the truth! Bah!

Molly (*aside to the audience, giving them the thumbs up*) Thanks, folks!

Teddy bounces on L

Teddy Hallo, Mum!

Molly (*groaning*) Oh, that's torn it!

Tightwad (*to Teddy, with suspicion*) Who are you?

Teddy Me? I'm Teddy Cod ....
Molly (*suddenly gripping her leg and howling in pain*) Ahhhhgh!!
Ooooow!!
Teddy Mum! What's the matter?
Molly (*massaging her leg*) It's me old trouble again! One of me muscular
chasms ! You'd better take me 'ome!
Teddy (*indicating the cottage*) But we're right outside our —
Molly (*howling again*) Oooow!! (*Clinging to Teddy*) Take me 'ome,
Teddy! You know what Dr (*local*) said. (*Acting weak*) I must 'ave
complete rest when I get one of me turns! Take me 'ome ... (*anything
but weak*) now!! (*Aside to Teddy*) It's 'im, you twit! Old Tightwad!
Teddy (*cottoning on*) Oh! ... er ...Yes, let's get you home right away,
Mummy. I'll give you a nice rub down and a full massacre!

Teddy assists Molly towards the L *exit. Tightwad stops them*

Tightwad Just a minute! You still haven't told me your name.
Teddy It's Teddy Smith. (*Or perhaps the surname of a local character
can be used*)
Tightwad Are you sure it's not Coddle?
Teddy 'Course it's not twaddle! It's the truth!
Molly (*to Teddy*) 'E's lookin' for someone called Molly Coddle. D'you
know the woman?
Teddy Yes! I've just seen her going into the (*local pub*)!
Molly There! That proves I'm not Molly Coddle! You'd never catch me
in *that* dive! (*To the audience*) Not after chuckin' out time, anyway!
Tightwad I'll go there at once! This time I'll catch her! (*He rushes to
the exit* R)

Cissie enters R, *still wearing the stupid hat*

Tightwad pulls up short

On seeing Cissie, Molly roars with laughter

Molly Ha! Ha! Ha! Look! It's the reject from (*local garden centre*)
again! Ha! Ha! Ha!
Cissie (*to Tightwad*) That nathty woman ith laughing at my hat!
Tightwad (*looking at the hat in disgust*) I'm not surprised! Fifty pounds
for a flowerpot!

More laughter from Molly. She holds her sides and doubles over

Cissie Make her thtop laughing at me, Uncle Tituth!

Molly suddenly stops laughing and gulps. She and Teddy react

Molly *Uncle?!*
Teddy (*aside to Molly*) Oh, no! I told her who you are!

Molly and Teddy edge towards the L exit during the following

Tightwad (*to Cissie, eager to be gone*) I haven't got the time! I must find Molly Coddle!
Cissie But — *that'th* her! (*Pointing to Molly*) *That'th* Molly Coddle! *He* told me tho!
Tightwad (*turning, with a roar*) *What!!*
Molly *Abandon ship!!*

Molly and Teddy run L

Some of the Villagers enter L, preventing Molly's and Teddy's escape

Molly and Teddy run R, but Tightwad and Cissie are waiting there. Tightwad grabs them by their collars

Tightwad Molly Coddle! At last! (*He gives a triumphant, miserly laugh*)

Goody and the rest of the Villagers enter R

Goody What's going on? ... What's happening?
Molly Oh, Goody! I've been grabbed by the creditors!
Goody (*to Tightwad*) I assume you are Mr Tightwad. Our new landlord.
Tightwad You assume correctly.
Cissie (*nastily*) And *I'm* hith nieth. Nah! (*She pokes her tongue out at Goody*)
Goody Is it really necessary to keep hold of them like that?
Tightwad (*releasing them*) Not any more. (*To Molly*) I know who you are — *now!*
Molly (*suddenly gripping her leg and howling*) Ooooow!!
Tightwad And you can stop that playacting! I'll give you something real to scream about!
Molly (*nervously*) W — What?

Tightwad (*producing a very long piece of paper*) This!

Molly It's his bill from Oddbins!

Tightwad (*waving it*) It is a rent demand. A demand for rent that you have not paid for years. It amounts to the sum of — *two hundred pounds!*

Everyone reacts — not least the Coddle family

Tightwad (*to Molly*) Have you got the money? Can you pay it?

Molly Can Jordan jump up and down without givin' 'erself a black eye? What d'you think?! Do I look like (*topical or local wealthy person*)?!

Tightwad Then you leave me no alternative. If you cannot pay the two hundred pounds by today, I will have my bailiffs throw you and your family out of this cottage!

There is a horrified reaction from the others. Goody joins Molly and Teddy, and they form a forlorn little group. Cissie is revelling in their misery

Tightwad (*to Molly*) Well? Have you anything to say to me?

Molly Yes — plenty! But we've got little kiddies in!

Tightwad Bah! If you can't produce the money by six o'clock you will be thrown out into the street! What a pity it isn't snowing! Hee! Hee! Hee!

Tightwad exits R, cackling and rubbing his hands in true miserly fashion

Molly and Teddy let out pitiful wails, and Goody tries to comfort them. Cissie is enjoying this enormously

Cissie Nah! That'll teach you to make fun of my lovely hat! I don't thee you laughing now! Nah!

Cissie pokes her tongue out at them, then the audience, then exits R

The Villagers commiserate with the family, then exit in various directions

Molly (*putting her arms around Goody and Teddy, sadly*) I'm sorry, kids! A fine mother I've turned out to be! I've made you poor and 'omeless! From now on we'll be livin' in squalor.

Teddy It could be worse, we could be livin' in (*local place*). Cheer up, Mum. You know the old saying — every cloud has a torn lining, and there's always a light at the end of the funnel.

Simon enters L. *He has obviously heard of their bad news*

Simon Hallo. I was on my way here when I heard the news. I'm really very sorry. I wish I had the two hundred pounds to give you.
Goody I wish you had as well, Simon.

There is a magical effect. The lighting changes slightly, and strange sounds are faintly heard. (See Production Notes) The four react, and look about them in puzzlement. Normal service is then resumed!

Goody What on earth was that?
Molly Did you see it an' all? Oh, thank goodness! I thought I was 'avin' illuminations.
Teddy It was probably the (*local reference*) playin' up again!

A commotion is heard, and the Villagers rush on in great excitement. The 1st Villager is waving a raffle ticket in one hand, and a wad of bank notes in the other

1st Villager Simon! Simon! You won't believe your luck! You won't believe it!
Simon What?
1st Villager You've just won first prize in the raffle! Two hundred pounds! (*He hands Simon the ticket and notes*)
Simon (*aghast*) Two hundred pounds!
Molly (*to the audience, if there is a raffle held during the production*) Don't you lot get any ideas! The first prize 'ere is a cuddly toy! (*If there is not* ——) Well! I'll go to the foot of our stairs!
Simon (*holding out the notes to Goody*) Here you are, Goody. It looks like our wish has come true. Now I *do* have two hundred pounds to give you.
Goody But —— I was only joking. I can't take your money, Simon.
Simon (*to Goody*) A few seconds ago I didn't have the money. I shan't miss it. To you it means keeping a roof over your head. Please take it.
Goody Well ... if you're sure. (*She takes the money*) Thank you, Simon. (*She kisses his cheek*) Mum, aren't you going to thank Simon?
Molly You bet I am! Come 'ere, you lifesaver!

Molly hugs and kisses Simon. Teddy moves in to do the same, but Molly holds him back. Goody gives her the money

Molly Now I can pay old Tightpants! (*To an elderly Villager*) Run and fetch 'im!

The Villager heads for the exit R at a "run"

Well, do the best you can!

The Villager exits during the following

(*To all, overjoyed*) Oh! Who'd 'ave believed our luck, eh! If I didn't know better, I'd say it was magic!

Song 7

A jolly song and dance for Principals and Chorus

After the number, Tightwad and Cissie enter R. The elderly Villager returns and joins the others

Molly hides the money behind her back

Molly (*now full of bravado*) Here they are! Mr Grumpy and Little Weed!
Tightwad (*to Molly*) I am informed that you have miraculously acquired the two hundred pounds you owe me! Is this true?
Molly Yep! (*She produces the wad of notes and waves it in his face*)

The effect on Tightwad is electrifying! He drools, twitches, then holds out a grasping hand

Tightwad Give it to me! *Give it to me! I want it!*
Molly (*to the audience*) Oh, girls! I 'aven't 'eard *those* words for years! (*She gives him the money*)

Tightwad flicks the wad, doing a rapid count-up

It's all there. I 'aven't dropped one!

Tightwad pockets the money and turns to leave. Cissie stops him

Cissie Uncle Tituth. Aren't you forgetting thomething?

Tightwad What?
Cissie I bet the hathn't paid — *thith week'th* rent!

Molly and the others react

Tightwad Ah! Yes! You're right, Cissie. She *hasn't!* (*Going to Molly, with outstretched hand*) This week's rent, if you please! Twenty pounds!
Molly But — I 'aven't got it!
Tightwad Then the situation is as before! If you cannot produce the money by six o clock today, you will be thrown out!

Tightwad exits R with a miserly laugh

Cissie is revelling in the return of the Coddles' misery. She laughs, pokes her tongue out at them, then skips out after Tightwad

Molly (*wailing in despair*) Oh, no! Back to square one again! (*To Simon, hopefully*) Hey! You didn't buy any more raffle tickets, did ya?
Simon (*shaking his head, sadly*) I'm sorry.
Teddy We only need twenty pounds. (*Indicating the Villagers*) Per'aps our friends here will have a whip round for us.
Molly (*brightening*) You're right, Teddy! I'm sure they will. (*To the Villagers, over-pleasantly*) Now then, all you dear friends and *lovely* neighbours! Who'd like to help us out?
1st Villager (*eager to be gone*) Oh, dear! Is that the time?

The 1st Villager hurries out

2nd Villager (*following suit*) I think I left a tap running!
3rd Villager I've just remembered something!
Other Villagers Me too! Yes! Better go! Bye! (*etc.*)

All the Villagers beat hasty exits in various directions

Molly Well! How's that for community spirit! (*To the audience*) I don't suppose one of you'd like to ...
Teddy You can't ask *them* for money, Mum! They've had to fork out enough already!
Molly You're right! (*O.T.T. dramatic*) Come, my children! Let us pack our few meagre belongings, and prepare to be cast out into the cold, cold streets! (*She goes to make a dramatic exit into the cottage, but misjudges the door and hits the wall*)

Molly goes into the cottage, trying to retain her dignity

Teddy (*to the audience*) She's good, y'know. They don't call her the
Judi Dench of (*local place*) for nothin'!

Teddy exits into the cottage

Simon (*to Goody*) Don't worry. I'm going home to raid my piggy bank
for the twenty pounds.
Goody Thank you, Simon.

They embrace, and Simon exits L

Goody goes into the cottage

A slight pause, then Rolo and Polo creep on R

Polo (*looking across*) Do you think Goody lives in that cottage over
there?
Rolo There's only one way to find out. We'll go and knock.
Polo Coo! I wish I had a brain like yours!
Rolo *Any* sort of brain would be a improvement!
Polo Yeah! (*Double take*) Wot?
Rolo Let's get on with it!
Polo Before we do — just how are we gonna persuade Goody to give
us the shoes?
Rolo We'll tell her the truth.
Polo About sinister Septica?
Rolo We needn't mention *her*. We'll just tell Goody that we've come
to take the shoes back to their rightful owner. I'm sure she's a very
honest person and will give them to us without question.
Polo Yeah! Lead on!

They head towards the cottage

Cissie enters R, *unseen by Rolo and Polo. She sees the curious pair,
and stands watching them*

Polo comes to a sudden halt

Polo Hey! I've just had a thought!
Rolo This is no time to start new hobbies!
Polo Suppose Goody's discovered that the shoes have got magic
powers!

Cissie reacts. All ears, she moves a little closer

Polo If she's found out all her wishes will come true when she's wearing them, she might not want to give 'em back.
Rolo Listen. If she's discovered *that,* why d'you think she's still living in a place like *this?*
Polo True. She'd be livin' in (*local place*)! Lead on!

They start towards the cottage again

Cissie (*to the audience, excitedly*) Magic thooth! (*Calling to the Duo*) Exthooth me!

Rolo and Polo stop and turn. They are startled at the sight of her

Polo Yaagh! It's a giant fruit salad!

Cissie moves very close to them. She is the picture of innocence

Cissie I'm Thithie. Can I help you? Can I be of any athithtanth?

There is comic business as Rolo and Polo react to her watery lisp

Cissie Are you looking for thomeone?
Polo (*aside to Rolo, pushing him in front*) You talk to 'er! I had a shower last week!
Rolo (*to Cissie*) We are looking for someone called Goody.
Cissie Goody Coddle? Oh, the doth'nt live here. The liveth thomewhere elth!
Rolo (*wiping his eyes*) Really?
Cissie Yeth! The liveth in Thickamore Threet!
Rolo Sycamore Street?
Cissie (*very juicy*) Thath what I thed! Thickamore Threet! Number thickthty-thickth!
Rolo (*to Polo*) Did you hear that?
Polo (*nodding*) And felt it! (*He wipes his eyes*)
Rolo (*to Cissie*) Thank you ... We'll try there ... Thank you. (*Aside to Polo*) Come on, before we drown!

Rolo and Polo exit DL, *still wiping their faces*

As soon as they are out of sight, Cissie turns to the audience

Cissie (*with an unpleasant chuckle*) Hee! Hee! That thoppy Goody hath got magic thooth, and the doeth'nt know it! *I'm* going to have thoth magic thooth! All for mythelf! Tho there! (*She pokes her tongue out at the audience, then goes to the cottage and knocks on the door*)

Goody opens the door, and steps out

Cissie is all smiles and innocence

Goody (*surprised, but not hostile*) Oh! ... It's you.
Cissie (*with sickening sweetness*) Hallo, Goody.

Molly comes out of the cottage, followed by Teddy

Molly Who is it, Goody? Oh! (*She sees Cissie. Defiantly hostile*) It's that pot-bound petunia again! What do *you* want? Come to gloat, 'ave ya?!
Cissie Oh, no. I've come to thay how thorry I am for what'th happened.
Teddy That's very nice of you. Ta.
Molly (*to Teddy*) Oy, you! Stop cavortin' with the enemy! (*To Cissie*) Are you 'avin' us on?
Goody I think Cissie means it, mum.
Cissie (*butter wouldn't melt*) Yeth, I do. I want uth to be friendth.
Teddy That's fine by me!
Cissie (*pointedly*) Me and Goody, I mean!
Teddy (*disappointedly*) Oh!
Goody Well, there's no reason why we shouldn't be friends. You can't help having a nasty old uncle.
Cissie Oh, good! (*Taking Goody's arm*) Now that we're friendth, Goody, I muth thay I like your thooth.

They admire the shoes

Will you let *me* have them?
Goody Well, they don't actually belong to ——
Cissie I'll *buy* them from you.
Goody I ——
Molly (*cutting in*) 'Ow much?
Goody (*taking Molly aside*) Mum! They aren't mine to sell, remember?
Molly But this is our chance to pay old Tightwad! Ask 'er for the twenty quid!

Goody Mum ——
Molly Go on! To keep a roof over our 'eads, and a floor under our other
  bits! Just think of yer poor, pathetic brother! (*Pointing to Teddy*) Look
  at' im! Pathetic!
Goody Oh ... (*Giving in*) All right.
Molly Attagirl! Ask 'er for forty quid while you're at it.
Goody I won't. (*Turning to Cissie*) All right. If you can persuade your
  uncle to forget the twenty pounds my mother owes him, you can have
  the shoes.
Cissie Tha'th eathy! (*She goes* R, *and calls off*) Uncle Tituth!! Uncle
  Tituth!!
Molly Uncletitus? Ugh! It sounds like a nasty complaint!

A disgruntled Tightwad stomps on R

Teddy *It is!*
Tightwad What's all the shouting about?
Cissie (*taking his arm; very affectionately*) Uncle Tituth — *dear*. I want
  you to do thomthing for me.
Tightwad (*with suspicion*) What?
Cissie I want you to buy me a pair of thooth.
Tightwad (*exploding*) Buy you shoes! I most certainly will not! I've
  already bought you that ridiculous hat! No! You won't get another
  penny out of me!
Cissie But you won't have to part with any money, Uncle Tituth. It'th
  Good'th thooth I want. If you forget about the twenty poundth rent
  they owe you, the'll let me have them.
Tightwad Never!
Cissie (*in a sing-song voice*) Inheritanth!

Tightwad is in turmoil for a moment, then grumpily gives in

Tightwad Oh! ... Very well!
Cissie Thooper! (*To Goody, all friendliness vanished*) Give me thoth
  thooth! (*Clinging to Tightwad, she quickly takes off her own shoes*)
Molly (*to Goody*) Get 'em off! Get 'em off! Before old Titus changes
  'is mind!

*Rather sadly, Goody takes off her shoes. Cissie thrusts her own shoes at
Tightwad, then snatches the shoes from Goody. She eagerly thrusts her
feet into them. They prove to be a tight fit, and cause her many painful
contortions*

(*Calling out front*) Is there a tyre lever in the house?

Finally, Cissie manages to get the shoes on. She walks up and down with some difficulty, but pretends that there is no problem

Tightwad   Twenty pounds for something that doesn't even fit! Ridiculous! *Bah!!*

Tightwad stomps out R, *grumbling to himself. Molly and Goody go into the cottage*

Teddy lingers, watching Cissie

Teddy (*trying his best*) D'you know, in that hat and those shoes you look just like (*current model / film star*)!

Cissie gives him a ferocious glare

I know ... Go away!

Teddy goes into the cottage, crestfallen

With the coast clear, Cissie now comes forward to gloat to the audience

Cissie Hee! Hee! The magic thooth are mine! All mine! I can't wait to try out their powerth! Now — what thall I wi'th for? Money? ... No, I can alwayth get money from thupid old uncle! Beauty? ... No, I thertainly don't need that! I'm beautiful enough already! Now, what ... ? (*Suddenly struck by an idea*) I know what I'll with for! Yeth! Here go'th! (*She looks down at the shoes, then shuts her eyes tightly*) I wi'th that Thimon woth in love with *me* and not with Goody!

The magical effect happens again. This time it is dark and sinister, with thunder and lightning, and eerie sounds. (See Production Notes)

The Villagers rush on from various directions in a state of bewilderment. Molly, Goody and Teddy rush from the cottage at the same time. Goody is still barefoot

They all look about them in utter dismay

Molly Crikey! (*TV weather presenter*) didn't forecast this!

The magical effect ends, and things return to normal

Simon enters L. *He sees Cissie*

Simon (*exclaiming, in a voice filled with passion*) Cissie! My sweetheart!
My darling!

*Simon rushes across to Cissie, throws his arms around her and embraces
her. She is surprised, but nonetheless delighted. The others are just plain
gobsmacked*

Cissie (*to the audience, over Simon's shoulder*) It worked!
Simon (*holding her at arms' length, and gazing at her adoringly*) Oh!
My beloved! (*He embraces her again*)

*The others cannot believe their eyes and ears. Molly is suddenly
galvanized into action. She grabs Goody by the hand, and rushes down
to Simon. Teddy and the Villagers gather around*

Molly Hey, you! (*Tapping Simon on the shoulder*) What d'you think yer
playin' at? Stop fawnin' over that floppy flowered floozy! I thought
you were supposed to be in love with our Goody!
Simon (*turning to Molly, quite unmoved*) Not any more.

There's a reaction from all the others

Goody (*dismayed and upset, to say the least*) But, Simon ... What have
I done?
Simon Nothing at all. It's quite strange. I was on my way here when I
suddenly realized that I was really in love with Cissie. It just came to
me out of the blue. It hit me like a thunderbolt.
Molly Not as 'ard as I'd hit ya! Oh, 'ow can you do this to my poor little
girl! Look at 'er! She's desiccated!
Simon I'm very sorry, but that's the way it is. (*He turns back to gaze
adoringly at Cissie*) From now on Cissie is the only girl in the world
for me.
Cissie (*to Goody*) Nah! (*She pokes her tongue out at her*)

Bursting into tears, Goody runs out L

Cissie laughs, then she and Simon go into a soppy embrace

Molly (*fuming*) Gerrrgh! (*To the audience*) Men!!
Teddy Poor Goody! Still, you know the old saying: it's better to have
loved and lost than never to have counted your chickens before they
cross the road!

Molly drags Teddy out L, *exasperated*

Cissie Oh, Thimon! I'm tho happy! Let'th thing thomething to thelebrate!

Song 8

Song and dance for Cissie and Simon. Despite the situation, the Villagers join in with enthusiasm. The number ends with a tableau, Cissie and Simon embracing in the centre, with the Villagers grouped around them. Over Simon's shoulder, Cissie is making faces and poking her tongue out at the audience

The CURTAIN *falls*

ACT II
Scene 1

Near the village

Tabs, or the frontcloth as ACT I, Scene 2

The opening sequence of this scene is performed in the style of an old silent film. (The following are only suggestions. Individual directors will have their own ideas on how to present the sequence. See Production Notes)

When the Curtain *rises, the stage is empty*

Teddy enters DR. *He carries six large cards with captions written on both sides of each. He holds up a card to show the caption: "THE STORY SO FAR". Unfortunately, it is upside down! After protests from the audience, he turns it the right way up. He then turns the card over to show the caption: "POOR GOODY. AHH!"*

The tune of "Hearts and Flowers" plays

Goody enters L. *Still barefoot, she presents a woeful picture of the heartbroken heroine*

Teddy encourages the audience to sigh for her. He then holds up a card to show the caption: "HER POOR OLD MUM"

The tune of "Home Sweet Home" plays

Molly enters L. *She sees Goody, exhibits exaggerated motherly concern, then goes to comfort her*

Teddy turns the card over to show the caption: "HER HANDSOME BROTHER. HURRAY!"

The tune of "For he's a jolly good fellow" plays. Teddy swaggers over to comfort Goody

Goody exits L, *in tears. Molly, again showing exaggerated concern, follows her out. She ruins the dramatic effect by bumping into the proscenium arch on the way!*

Teddy moves DL, *and holds up a card to show the caption: "THE WICKED LANDLORD! BOO! HISS!"*

Suitable villain music plays

Tightwad enters R. *He rubs his hands together and sneers at the audience in classic miserly fashion*

Teddy encourages the audience to boo and hiss

Tightwad exits R

Teddy turns the card over to show the caption: "HIS NASTY NIECE! BOO!"

Suitable "Vamp" music plays

Cissie slinks on R

Teddy encourages the audience to boo and hiss. Cissie responds by making faces and poking her tongue out. She then shows off her shoes, and mimes making her magic wish

Suitable "heroic" chords play

Simon strides on R

Teddy holds up a card to show the caption: "THE HERO!"

Simon sees Cissie, and responds with overwhelming passion. To the theme from "Love story", they "run" towards each other in slow motion. They meet in a soppy embrace

Simon and Cissie exit R

Teddy turns the card over to show the caption: "THE ALSO-RANS"

Suitable music for the Elf Cobbler and Septica plays

The Elf Cobbler runs across from R *to* L. *He reacts in horror, turns tail, and runs out* R

Septica limps on L

Teddy holds up a card to show the caption: "BOO! HISS!"

Septica reacts to the audience, then limps off R

Rolo and Polo enter L

Teddy turns the card over to show the caption: "HURRAY!"

Rolo and Polo wave to the audience, then run out R

Teddy holds up a card to show the caption: "A QUICK RECAP"

Suitable "chase" music plays

The whole sequence is repeated, but this time in fast forward mode. Characters appear and disappear in rapid succession, all desperately trying to remain in character. Teddy gets into a hopeless mess with his cards. The music increases in speed, and they attempt an even faster action replay! This time there is total chaos and confusion! Finally, Teddy takes a huge card from the wings, and holds it up. It bears the caption:"CUT!" The music and the flickering light effect stop abruptly

Those left on stage, stagger or crawl away into the wings

Teddy turns the card over to show the caption: "BACK TO THE PLOT"

Teddy stumbles out L

Rolo and Polo enter from DR

Rolo (*to the audience*) I've been hoodwinked!
Polo That's why he's walkin' a bit funny.
Rolo No! I'm talking about that girl in the silly hat! That Cissie! She sent on a wild goose chase! She *said* Goody lived in Sycamore Street.
Polo She didn't *say* it! She *sprayed* it! (*Mimicking the watery lisp*) Number thickthty-thickth!

Rolo There's no Sycamore Street in the village! It doesn't exist!

Polo She told us a porky pie!

Rolo *Why* did she do that? *Why* did she lie? *Why* didn't she want us to find Goody? *Why?*

Polo *Why* does a brown cow always give white milk when it only eats green grass?

Rolo Be serious!

Polo Perhaps our friends out there know the answer. They've seen the bits we haven't seen. Ask them.

Rolo A good idea. (*To the audience*) Do you know why Cissie didn't want us to find Goody?

"Yes!" from the audience

Polo Has it got something to do with the magic shoes?

"Yes!" from the audience

Rolo Does Goody know they're *magic* shoes?

"No!" from the audience

Polo Does *Cissie* know they're magic shoes?

"Yes!" from the audience

Rolo Please don't tell us Cissie's got the shoes!

"Yes!" from the audience

Both *Oh, no!*

Rolo And has she used their magic powers yet?

"Yes!" from the audience

Polo What's she done?

"Made Simon fall in love with her," etc. from the audience

What a rotten, sneaky thing to do!

Rolo It certainly is. Poor Goody.

Polo I wouldn't mind taking that Cissie back to old Septica. She deserves to get punished for what she's done to Goody.

Rolo (*struck by an idea*) Wait! That's it! We don't have to pretend we disposed of Goody. We'll just pretend that Cissie is Goody!

Polo (*puzzled*) Come again?

Rolo Septica doesn't know what Goody looks like, does she?

Polo No.

Rolo There you are then! If we don't tell her any different, she'll think Cissie is Goody.

Polo And *she'll* get punished instead! Great! (*To the audience*) You'd like to see that horrible Cissie get punished, wouldn't you?

"Yes!" from the audience

I thought you would.

Rolo We'd better get on with it. The hour must be nearly up. We don't want Septica coming after us.

Polo Oh, I reckon she was bluffing. She won't come here herself. Not with her bunions and blisters! (*He walks about, comically mimicking Septica's painful limp*)

Septica limps on DL, *unseen by the duo*

Septica stands watching Polo's antics. The audience will be shouting warnings. Rolo sees Septica, and tries to warn Polo, but he is having too much fun limping about to take notice. He limps right up to Septica before he becomes aware of her presence. When he does, he tries to disguise the limp with a few dance steps. He dances back DR *where he cowers behind Rolo*

Septica (*limping towards them with an angry snarl*) Your time is up, you incompetent fools! Why have you not returned with my precious shoes? I warned you what would happen if I had to come here in person! You have forced me to make the ~~journey in~~ these appalling shoes! Every step has been atrocious agony to me! But *my* pains will be nothing compared to the ones I shall inflict on *you!*

Rolo (*cringing*) I ... I do apologize, your spitefulness.

Polo D-d-ditto, your deviousness.

Septica I am still waiting for an answer! Why have you not returned with my shoes? Where are they? I want my lovely comfy shoes! I want them — now! (*Again, she makes the grave mistake of stamping her foot. She yells, and hops about in agony*)

Polo gives a nervous giggle. Septica turns on him with a vicious snarl

Rolo We know exactly where they are. In fact, we were just on our way to get them. (*To Polo*) Weren't we?

Polo Was we? ... Oh, yes! ... We was!.

Septica I see. And what of the girl who stole them? What of the wretched Goody!

Polo Oh, she hasn't got 'em anymo...

Rolo (*quickly cutting in*) Fear not! We will be bringing her also! (*Pretending to be evil and sinister*) And then, your vileness, you can inflict the painful punishment she so richly deserves!

Septica (*with relish*) Ah, yes! I am really looking forward to that! (*An evil laugh*) Hee! Hee! Hee!

Rolo joins in with the evil laughter. He nudges Polo to participate in the villainy. When he does, it's so O.T.T. that the other two stop and stare at him. Finally, Rolo has to get him under control

Septica massages her painful feet

Rolo (*to Septica, very servile*) As you are obviously in great discomfort, I suggest you retire to some quiet spot and await our return with your shoes and the girl.

Polo Yeah! Pop into the (*local pub*) and put yer trotters up.

Septica Are you mad! It's the (*local high class hotel/club*) or nothing for me! So be it! I will wait for you there. But I do not expect to wait for long. If I have to come looking for you a second time ... (*She advances on them, threateningly*)

Rolo (*cringing*) W-we'll be no time at all, your impatientness.

Polo We'll move with the speed of light ale!

Septica Then what are you waiting for! (*Yelling at them*) *Get me my shoes!*

They rush past her for the DL exit. As they go, Polo manages to tread on Septica's foot. She yells in agony and hops about

Rolo and Polo exit

Septica hobbles painfully DS to address the audience

Septica Are you laughing at me? Do you find it funny? Well, you won't find it so funny when I've got my precious magic shoes back! Oh, no! You won't be laughing then! You'll all be *screaming!* (*An evil laugh*) Hee! Hee! Because as soon as I've dealt with Goody, I will be coming to get *you!* Oh, yes, I will!

A routine with the audience follows. It ends with her making the same mistake of stamping her foot

Septica hobbles out DR, *shaking her fist and snarling at the audience*

The Lights fade to Black-out

Music is played to cover the scene change

SCENE 2

Outside Molly's cottage

As ACT I, SCENE 3

The Lights come up. Molly, Teddy and the Villagers are discovered. Teddy is looking off R

Molly (*seeing the audience, and waving*) 'Allo, folks! Hi, kids! Nice to see you're back. (*To someone*) Nice to see your front!
Teddy (*to the others*) Look out! Goody's coming!
Molly (*to the Villagers*) Now remember, you lot — (*to the audience*) and you, folks! Our Goody's bin dumped by that so and so Simon! We've got to try to cheer the poor girl up. (*To the conductor/pianist*) Let's 'ave somethin' nice and jolly.

"The Funeral March" is played. After protests from Molly and the others, a jolly intro is played

Song 9

A jolly song and dance for Molly, Teddy and the Villagers

Goody enters R, *still barefoot, and looking sad and forlorn*

The others attempt to raise her spirits with the song. Teddy and Molly try to make her laugh with comical antics. Goody just manages a faint smile. The number ends with them all gathered around her for a big showbiz finish

Goody Thank you, everyone. I do appreciate you're trying to cheer me up, but ... but .... (*She breaks down, and starts to cry*)
Molly (*putting a comforting arm around Goody*) Oh, there, there! Don't upset yerself again, lovie.

Goody (*tearfully*) Oh, why did he do it, Mum? *Why?*

Molly I don't know. That's men for ya! They lead you up the garden path, then dump you on the nearest compost heap!

Goody But I don't understand how it happened. It wasn't as if we'd had a row or anything. One minute he's in love with me, and the next ——

Molly He's in love with that thoppy Thithie! It is weird. It's almost as if she'd put a magic spell on 'im.

Goody (*smiling in spite of everything*) Oh, Mum! Now you're being silly.

Molly Anyway, if that's 'is taste in women, you're well rid of 'im.

Villager You'll soon find someone else, Goody.

Teddy Yeah! You know the old saying: there's plenty more fish in the aquarium, and a rolling stone gathers no eggs in its basket!

Molly Teddy?

Teddy Yes, Mum?

Molly Sher up!

Teddy Yes, Mum.

Molly (*to Goody*) Come on. I'll make us a nice cuppa.

Goody If you don't mind, I'd rather like to be on my own for a while.

Molly 'Course, dear. (*To the Villagers*) You 'eard! (*A la Garbo*) She vonts to be alone!

The Villagers exit in various directions

Molly gives Goody a motherly kiss, then moves up to the cottage. Teddy lingers to talk to Goody

Teddy (*in an uneasy undertone*) Goody, I know you probably hate Cissie at the moment, but ... er ...

Goody What is it, Teddy?

Teddy Y'see — I like her! There! I've said it. I can't help it. I just do. I was hoping she and I ... (*Sadly*) Well, it looks like you and me are in the same boat now, sis.

Goody (*genuinely sorry for him*) Oh, Teddy.

Teddy Ah, well! We mustn't be downhearted. We must look to the future. You know the old saying: tomorrow is another stitch in time!

Molly Oy! Scarlett O'Hara! *Come 'ere!*

Teddy runs across to the cottage, and Molly pushes him inside. She exits

Goody comes forward to sing of her lost love

Song 10

Solo for Goody

After the song, Cissie and Simon enter R. *They are holding hands and behaving all "lovey dovey", particularly Cissie. It must be remembered that she is still finding the shoes uncomfortable, but it is a small price to pay for Simon's attentions*

Goody sees them, and quickly makes for the cottage

Cissie (*eager to continue tormenting Goody; calling*) Hallo, Goody.
Goody (*stopping and turning; putting on a brave face*) Hallo.
Cissie What are you doing?
Goody Nothing.
Cissie (*nastily*) That'th what I thought. (*Cuddling up to Simon*) We've got thome thooper newth! Haven't we, thweetheart?
Simon Yes, darling.
Cissie Thall I tell her or will you?
Simon We've ——
Cissie (*she can't resist it!*) We've juth got engaged!

This is a bitter blow to Goody, but she bears it bravely

Engaged to be married! Ithn't that wonderful newth? (*Really rubbing salt into the wound*) Aren't you going to congratulate uth, Goody?

Goody bursts into tears and runs out L

Cissie derives great satisfaction from this, and conveys her delight to the audience. When they show their disapproval, she responds in her usual manner by poking her tongue out at them. She then cuddles up to Simon

Thimon?
Simon Yes, my love?
Cissie Now that we're engaged, there'th thomething you have to give me.
Simon (*the poor besotted fool*) Anything, my angel! Just name it! All I have in the world is yours!
Cissie Good. I want a ring. An engagement ring!
Simon (*not quite so besotted*) Ah ... yes. They're rather expensive, aren't they?

Cissie (*pouting*) You thaid you'd give me anything! You thaid you would!

Simon And I will, my sweet. I'll have to get a loan from the bank.

Cissie (*hustling him towards the exit* L) Yeth. You go and do that! And hurry back with a nithe big ring for your little Thithie. One with lot'th an' lot'th of thparkling diamondth on it!

Simon (*reacting, but trying to make light of it*) In that case I'll have to *rob* the bank!

They blow soppy kisses to each other

Simon exits L

Cissie (*to the audience, smugly*) He'th tho in love with me I can get him to do anything I want! The betht thing woth pinching him away from that thoppy Goody! I *really* enjoyed doing that! Ha! Ha! Ha! With theath magic thooth of mine, I can do *anything* I like! Oh, yeth, I can!

There is a routine with the audience

(*When it's run its course*) Just for that, I'm going to turn you all into nathty thlimy thlugth! Hee! Hee! Hee! (*She shuts her eyes tightly, preparing to make the wish*) I wi'th you were all …

Suddenly, Rolo and Polo enter R

Rolo *There she is!*
Polo *Grab her!*

They advance on Cissie. Startled, Cissie opens her eyes, sees them advancing, lets out a scream and runs away

Suitable chase music plays

The duo pursues Cissie around the stage, with much yelling and screaming from Cissie. Eventually, they succeed in catching her. She yells and struggles

Rolo (*to Polo, desperately*) I'll hold her! You get the shoes! Get the shoes!

There is comic business as Polo tries to grab one of Cissie's thrashing feet. He gets kicked over a couple of times. He manages to grab a foot, and starts pulling at the shoe

Tightwad rushes on R *followed by some of the Villagers. At the same time, Molly and Teddy rush from the cottage. More Villagers rush on* UL

There is general uproar

Tightwad		*Cissie!*
Molly	*(together)*	What's goin' on?!
Teddy		Oy! Leave 'er alone!

Alarmed, Rolo and Polo release Cissie, who falls to the ground

The Duo exits L *at a run*

Tightwad (*moving over to Cissie*) What on earth's going on, Cissie? Who were those two? Why were they trying to pull your shoes off?
Molly Perhaps it was Trinny and Susanna!
Teddy (*going to Cissie*) Let me help you up.
Cissie (*snapping at him*) Go away!

Teddy jumps back. Cissie gets to her feet. There is comic business as she adjusts her dress and hat

Tightwad (*to Cissie, impatiently*) Well? Why were they trying to take your shoes?
Molly It's the shoes our Goody found in the forest.
Tightwad The ones that cost me twenty pounds!
Teddy Why would anyone want to steal *them?*
Molly That's what I'd like to know!
Tightwad And me!

They all look at Cissie, waiting for an answer. Edged into a corner, she takes the only way out. She bursts into floods of tears! The others react

Cissie (*wailing*) Waaaaa!!!
Tightwad Oh, no! Not the waterworks again!
Cissie (*between sobs*) I wanna go home! Take me home, Uncle Tituth!
Tightwad Bah! I haven't got the time! Go home on your own!
Cissie (*wailing*) Waaaaa!!!
Teddy I'll take her home.
Molly You'll *what?*
Tightwad (*to Cissie*) There you are. He'll take you home. (*To Teddy*) And don't expect to be paid for doing it!

Tightwad stomps out

Molly Teddy Coddle! How could ya! Offerin' to see 'er 'ome, after she pinched our Goody's fella!

Teddy That wasn't Cissie's fault, Mum. She couldn't help it if Simon fell in love with her.

Molly I'm not so sure about that! I bet she encouraged 'im. (*At Cissie*) The lispin' Lolita!

Teddy Have a heart, Mum. Can't you see she's upset. How would *you* like it if two men held *you* down and tried to pull *your* shoes off?

Molly How d'you know they 'aven't! And that's another thing — *why* were they tryin' to nick 'er shoes? What's so special about 'em? Ask 'er that! Go on! Ask 'er!

Again Cissie resorts to tears

Cissie (*wailing*) Waaaaaa!!!

Molly Ohh! Take 'er away if you're goin' to! She's worse than (*current group/singer*)!

Teddy (*gallantly offering his arm to Cissie*) May I have the honour?

Ignoring him completely, Cissie flounces out R

Teddy is left gaping, with his arm still held out. Molly and the others laugh

Molly That'll teach ya — Sir Prancealot!

Teddy goes out R *with his arm still extended*

(*To the audience*) See how well I've brung my children up. Despite bein' a complete plonker, he 'as lovely manners. 'E's a right aristoprat. And his heart's in the right place — even if his brain isn't!

Molly exits into the cottage

Music

Goody enters L. *Still sad and forlorn, she sings a short reprise of Song 10 with the Villagers*

Reprise of Song 10

At the end of the number, the Lights fade to Black-out

Music is played to cover the scene change

SCENE 3

Near the village

Tabs, or the front cloth as ACT II, SCENE 1

The Lights come up

Rolo and Polo run on from DR. *They pause to get their breath back*

Polo You really messed that up, didn't you!

Rolo Me? I like that! You were supposed to be getting the shoes off her. All you did was keep falling over!

Polo That's because *you* didn't hold her properly. You should have held on to her firmly!

Rolo (*with disgust*) I didn't want to hold on to *any* part of her — let alone her firmly!

Polo (*grimacing*) Nor me! She's hardly Miss World, is she?

Rolo More like Miss Piggy, I'd say.

Polo Well, what are we gonna do now?

Rolo We shall have to try again. And somewhere where there aren't any people about.

Polo Like (*local place*), y' mean?

Rolo And we're going to have to do it quickly. Septica isn't going to wait in the (*local hotel/club*) forever!

Polo She's probably on her third gin and tonic by now! (*He does a comical impression of a tipsy, limping Septica*)

Rolo (*looking off* DR) Here she is!

Polo (*panicking*) Septica?

Rolo No! Cissie! She's coming this way. Now's our chance. We'll hide — and then grab her!

Polo Right! (*To the audience*) You won't warn her, will you?

Rolo (*to the audience*) No, you mustn't do that! Remember, we want to take her back to Septica, and pretend she's Goody.

Polo So none of that "he's behind you!" business.

Rolo They know that! They're not stupid.

Polo True! That's why they're down there, and we're up 'ere!

Rolo hauls Polo out DL

Cissie flounces on DR. *Teddy follows at a short distance, out of breath*

Teddy Hold on, Cissie! You're goin' too fast for me!
Cissie (*stopping and snapping at him*) Who thaid you could call me Thithie?
Teddy Well, I thought — as I'm seein' you home ...
Cissie And that'th *all* you're doing! Theaing me home. Don't get above yourthelf!
Teddy I'd need a ladder to do that! (*He guffaws at his joke*)

Cissie moves over to him, and the laughter dwindles into embarrassed silence

Cissie Tell me, were you born thupid, or did you have to take lethonth?
Teddy That's not a very nice thing to spray — I mean — say. I know I'm not clever, or handsome, but I do have feelings. (*Proudly*) I am a human being!
Cissie Huh! I'd like to thea a doctor'th report on that!
Teddy I might not have brains ——
Cissie There'th no *might* about it!
Teddy — or breeding ——
Cissie You thertainly wouldn't win any prizeth at Croftth!
Teddy — but I can be very loyal. For instance, if you and Simon were to split up, I'd be more than happy to take his place in your afflictions.
Cissie (*moving away, unable to believe her ears*) You? You think I'd have *you* for a boyfriend? An *ugly* looking thing like you!
Teddy Ah! You know the old saying: never judge a book by its rose-tinted spectacles, and beauty is only still waters running deep! (*Moving to her, earnestly*) Oh, Cissie! I know I could make you happy. What I'm trying to say is ...

Song 11

A comedy duet and dance for Teddy and Cissie. He passionately sings of his virtues, while she passionately sings of his faults. When they dance together, Teddy sees Fred and Ginger, while Cissie sees a wrestling match she means to win! The number ends with Teddy collapsing face down to the ground

Teddy (*getting to his knees*) There! That's how I feel about you!
Cissie And thith ith how I feel about *you!* (*She plants her foot on his bottom, and pushes him down again*) Now, go away, and leave me alone!

Teddy (*scrabbling to his feet*) But — I've got to see you home!
Cissie I thaid — (*roaring at him*) Go *away!*
Teddy (*backing away to* R) All right! I'll go! (*Downcast*) I know when I'm not wanted. (*To the audience*) You can't blame me for trying though, can you? You know the old saying: faint heart never made a silk purse out of a sow's ear!

Teddy looks at Cissie and gives a forlorn sigh. He encourages the audience to sigh with him, then exits DR

Rolo and Polo creep on DL. *They caution the audience to remain silent, then creep up behind the unsuspecting Cissie*

Cissie (*to the audience*) Who doth he think he ith? Thaying he'd like to be *my* boyfriend indeed! I'm much too good for the likth of him. He'th tho common and ——

The duo grabs her

Ahhhhgh!!
Rolo You're coming with us!
Polo Yeah! You're goin' daaaan!

Cissie lets out a scream. They drag her towards the exit DL

Teddy rushes on DR

Teddy Hey! Let her go! What's goin' on? Where are you taking Cissie?
Rolo To our mistress! To Septica, the Sorceress!
Polo (*with relish*) The *eeeevil* Sorceress!
Teddy But ... why? What's she going to do to Cissie?
Polo (*grimacing*) Believe me, you don't wanna to know! Ugh!
Cissie (*yelling in terror*) Waaagh!
Teddy But — what's she done?
Rolo She stole Septica's magic shoes!
Teddy (*in disbelief*) Magic shoes?
Polo (*pointing to Cissie's shoes*) Them ones!
Cissie (*wailing*) *I never!*
Teddy That wasn't her! That was my sister Goody! And she didn't actually *steal* them — she just sort of borrowed them.
Rolo It makes no difference. Cissie is wearing the shoes now. In Septica's eyes *she is* the thief, and she must be severely punished!
Cissie (*terrified*) Punithed?

Polo (*copying her lisp*) *Theverely!*

Cissie gets out an even louder wail

Teddy Don't upset yourself, Cissie. This is some sort of joke. Right, fellas? Where's the hidden camera? Where's (*TV reference*)?
Rolo I assure you, it's no joke.
Teddy (*laughing*) Oh, come off it! Magic shoes! An evil Sorceress! There's no such thing! (*To the audience*) Is there, folks?

"Oh, yes, there is!" from the audience

Oh, very good! They've got you in on the joke as well, have they! And the next thing you'll be telling me is that the evil Sorceress has just walked in!

Septica limps on DR

The audience will be shouting warnings to Teddy. The duo and Cissie react in silent dread

(*Cocky*) And she's standing right behind me, I suppose?

Septica moves behind Teddy

"Yes!" from the audience

Oh, come on! I'm not gonna fall for that one! I'm not that daft! Yell all you like, I'm not gonna look! (*He folds his arms*) No, definitely not!

Septica moves round to stand on his right. There is comic business as he gradually becomes aware of her

(*Nervously*) 'Afternoon. T-That lot t-thinks you're an evil s-s-sorceress.
Septica (*snarling at him*) I am!
Teddy (*recoiling* US) Yaaah!
Septica (*looking across*) Ah! Are those my precious shoes I see?
Rolo Yes, your fearfulness.

The duo pulls the terrified Cissie forward

Septica (*elated*) At last! At last! (*She limps across as fast as she can. She gazes on the shoes like a mother seeing her long lost child. Her gaze then travels to Cissie, and it becomes anything but motherly!*)

Teddy works his way R

So! This is the miserable wretch who stole my lovely shoes, is it? What have you to say for yourself, thief?

Cissie is too terrified to say anything

Well, I'll say one thing for you. You have much better taste in shoes than you do in hats! (*She cackles, then turns to the audience*) See! I can make jokes as well! Pretty funny, wasn't it?

There is by-play with the audience

(*To the duo*) Why aren't you laughing at my joke, fools?

Rolo and Polo give forced laughs. Septica raises her hand, and they stop instantly

Away with her! Take her to my domain in the depths of Fearsome Forest! (*With evil relish*) Later, I will devise a suitably agonizing punishment to inflict upon her!

The duo prepares to drag Cissie out. She lets out a despairing wail

Wait! First remove the shoes from her feet, and give them to me! I long for their comfortable caress. I have endured this agony long enough! Give me my shoes!

Rolo and Polo kneel beside Cissie, preparing to remove her shoes. Suddenly, Teddy springs across and stamps on Septica's toe. Yelling in agony, she hops away upstage. Teddy pushes over the startled Duo and grabs Cissie

Teddy runs out with Cissie DL

(*Hobbling downstage, in a frenzy of agony and rage*) After them! Don't let them get away! Get after them, you fools!

Rolo and Polo scrabble out DL

Septica remains C. She balances on one leg and nurses her injured foot

Teddy and Cissie run on DL, heading DR. They run past Septica, almost managing to knock her over, then run straight out DR

Recovering, Septica gingerly puts her foot to the ground

Rolo and Polo run on DL

Septica (*pointing* R) They went that way! *That way!*

Rolo and Polo run DR

Polo manages to tread on Septica's sore foot en route. *Yelling, she hops about on one leg holding the damaged foot*

Rolo and Polo exit DR

Teddy and Cissie run on DR, *heading* DL. *Again, they almost knock Septica over and run straight out* DL

In pursuit, Rolo and Polo run on from DR *and head* DL. *This time, Polo manages to tread on Septica's other foot! They run straight out* DL

Septica hobbles out after them, yelling with rage and pain

Cissie runs on from DR *to* C. *She is in a state of panic. She is barefoot, and carrying the shoes*

Cissie I mutht get rid of theath thooth! I don't care if they *are* magic! I don't want that horrible perthon doing nathty things to me. I didn't take them! It wath Goody! Thith ith all her fault! The'th the one who ought to be punithed, not me! (*She looks* DR) Here thea cometh now!

Goody enters DR. *She is still barefoot*

(*Rushing straight to Cissie; hastily*) I don't want theath thooth anymore! You can have them back! (*She thrusts the shoes into Goody's hands*)

Cissie runs out DR

Goody (*to the audience*) That's odd. I wonder why she doesn't want them any more? Never mind. I'm so pleased to have them back. Once I was Goody *Two* Shoes. Then I was Goody *No* Shoes. And now — (*slipping the shoes on*) I'm Goody *Two* Shoes again! (*She does a few dance steps*) It's really nice to have them back. (*Sadly*) I *wish* I had the love of Simon back as well.

There is a magical effect; a lighting change and magical sounds. Goody is too busy admiring the shoes to notice. The effect ends

   Simon enters DL

Simon (*rapturously*) Goody!
Goody (*startled*) Oh!
Simon (*rushing to her with open arms*) My darling!
Goody (*backing away, confused*) I — I don't understand ...
Simon What is there to understand? I love you! It's as simple as that.
Goody But ... What about Cissie?
Simon Oh, that was a mistake. I suddenly realized it as I was on my way here with the engagement ring I bought for her. (*He takes out a ring box and opens it*) Look. I want *you* to have it now, Goody. Because it's you I truly love. (*He moves towards her*)

Goody dodges past him, and runs to the other side of the stage. Naturally, the poor girl is confused, upset and angry

What's wrong? I thought you'd be pleased.
Goody (*fighting back tears*) Pleased! Oh, how could you!
Simon But ...
Goody (*letting him have it*) Just who do you think you are? First you're in love with me, then you're in love with Cissie! Then you're in love with me again! You can't play fast and loose with people's emotions like that. It isn't fair!
Simon (*moving towards her*) Goody ——
Goody Don't come near me!
Simon (*halting in his tracks*) If you'll just listen to me ——
Goody I never want to listen to you again. How can I trust a word you say after what you've done. Leave me alone!

Goody bursts into tears and runs out DL

Simon (*following her to the exit*) Goody ... Wait ...

   Cissie enters from DR

Cissie (*seeing him and letting out a delighted squeal*) Thimon! (*She runs across and hugs Simon*)

Simon is too preoccupied to take any notice of her, and continues to look off L

What'th the matter, thweetheart? Aren't you pleathed to thee your little Thithie?

Simon takes no notice

Thimon? (*She gives him a hefty shake*) *Thimon!*
Simon (*giving her the briefest of glances*) Oh ... Hallo. (*He goes back to looking off* L)
Cissie (*with a pout*) Thimon! Why are you being tho ... (*She sees the ring box he is still holding, and gives a squeal of delight*) Oooh! Ith that my engagement ring? Oooh! Let me thea it! (*She reaches for the box*)

Simon holds it away from her

Simon That's not for you!
Cissie Not for me? But ...
Simon Look ... er ... I'm afraid I have some bad news for you, Cissie. I'm not in love with you any more.
Cissie (*aghast*) Not in love with me?
Simon No. I'm in love with Goody.
Cissie *Goody?*
Simon Er — yes — again. (*Looking off* L) I really must go after her. (*He starts for the exit, then turns back as an afterthought*) Bye.

Simon runs out DL

Cissie just stands there, completely gob-smacked. She then starts to wail. It grows in volume like a siren

Molly rushes on DR

Molly (*shouting above the din*) Oy! Oy! Where's the fire?

Tightwad stumps on from DR

Tightwad Cissie ... (*To Molly*) What's the matter with the girl?
Molly Don't ask me! You'd better stop 'er or we'll get complaints from (*local gag*)!
Tightwad (*stomping over to Cissie*) Cissie! Stop that infernal racket! Stop it at once, I say!

But Cissie continues to wail

(*To Molly*) She won't stop! Can't *you* do something to stop her?
Molly (*rolling up her sleeve*) With pleasure! Out me way! (*With raised fist, she advances on Cissie*)

Suddenly, the wailing stops

Tightwad She's stopped.
Molly (*to the audience*) Shame!
Tightwad Cissie?
Cissie (*looking at him, in a daze*) Uh?
Tightwad What's the matter with you? What was all that caterwauling about?

Cissie explains. But it just comes out in a series of unintelligible wails, gurgles, sobs and sniffs

Molly (*to the audience*) That's about as clear as the (*topical gag*)!
Cissie (*a desperate wail*) Thimon!!

Cissie runs out DL, *wailing*

Tightwad follows her to the exit and looks off

Tightwad What's the matter with the confounded girl? She's just run into the forest after some young fella! Bah! I suppose I'd better go after her. I have to keep a close watch on my asset!

Tightwad stomps out DL, *grumbling*

Molly (*to the audience, moving* DC) 'E must 'ave eyes in the back of 'is 'ead to do that! I wonder what's 'appened to our Teddy? 'E was supposed to be seein' that walkin' water feature 'ome!

Teddy runs across the back from DR, *heading* DL, *closely pursued by Rolo and Polo*

Teddy (*yelling*) Muuuuuuuum!

Teddy, Rolo and Polo exit DL

Molly turns but Teddy, Rolo and Polo are out of sight

Molly (*to the audience*) That's funny! I could 'ave sworn I 'eard Teddy callin' to me.

Teddy, still pursued by Rolo and Polo, runs across the back from DL, *heading* DR

Teddy (*yelling*) Muuuuuuum!

Teddy, Rolo and Polo exit DR

Molly turns to look, but they have gone

Molly (*to the audience*) There it was again! Did you 'ear it? Was Teddy 'ere?

"Yes!" from the audience

Well, if you see 'im again, give me a shout, will ya?

Teddy and the duo run across from DR, *and out* DL. *The audience shouts to Molly. By the time she looks, they have gone*

(*To the audience*) Was it 'im?

"Yes!" from the audience

Are you sure?

Teddy and the duo run across from DL, *and out* DR. *The audience shouts. Molly repeats the business from before*

(*To the audience*) You're not shoutin' fast enough! You'll 'ave to be much quicker than that!

Teddy and the duo run across from DR *and out* DL. *The audience shouts. (Repeat this business for as long as desired)*

(*Finally, to the audience*) I think you lot are 'avin' me on! 'E wasn't there at all, was 'e?

"Yes!" from the audience

Oh, no, 'e wasn't!

This business continues. While Molly is engaged with the audience:

Teddy crawls in on all fours DL. *He is exhausted and unable to speak. He crawls to Molly, and tugs weakly at her dress. Eventually, she becomes aware of him, and hauls him to his feet*

Teddy Coddle! What are you playin' at?

Teddy can only gasp for breath

What's up with ya? I've warned you about smokin' them cabbage leaves!

Septica limps on DR, unseen by Molly

Teddy sees Septica, and tries to warn Molly. But he can only manage wheezes and gasps. Septica moves to Molly's R

(*To Teddy*) What are you tryin' to say? Pull yerself together! What is it?

Teddy points. Molly looks to where he is pointing. She sees Septica, and does a huge double take

Yaaagh!! *It's* (*current nasty*)!
Teddy *Run for it!*

Molly and Teddy rush to the DL exit, but pull up short as Rolo and Polo appear there

Septica *Seize them!*

The duo grab one each

(*Snarling at Teddy*) Where is that girl with my shoes? Tell me where she is, or I will make you suffer! You *and* this — ugly old hag!
Molly 'Ere! Not so much of the ugly! You're no (*current looker*) yerself! What girl are you talkin' about?
Septica The one with the silly voice, and the even sillier hat!
Molly Oh, you mean that awful Cissie. I can tell you where she is.
Teddy No, Mum ... !
Septica (*snarling at Molly*) Tell me! *Tell me!*
Molly All right! All right! Don't get yer perm in a pickle! She went into the forest.
Septica (*giving her fiendish laugh*) Hee! Hee! Hee!!
Molly (*to the audience*) I'll 'ave some of what she's drinkin'!
Septica Excellent! She has entered the Fearsome Forest! My domain! She will not escape from me there!
Molly What you gonna do to 'er when you catch 'er?

Septica (*with evil relish*) She will be severely punished!
Molly (*pleased*) Oh, great! Can I watch?
Septica I will let you do more than that. I will let you — *join* her!
Molly Smashin'! (*She reacts*) Eh?!
Septica The more the merrier. It would be a shame to waste the punishment on just one! (*Evil laugh*) Hee! Hee! Hee! (*To the duo*) Away with them! To the Fearsome Forest!

Rolo and Polo drag the whimpering pair out DL. *Septica limps out after them, snarling and sneering at the audience as she goes*

The Lights fade to Black-out

Sinister music plays to cover the scene change

SCENE 4

The Fearsome Forest

As ACT I, SCENE 1

The Lights come up. The Forest Demons are discovered. They perform a short reprise of their song and dance

Reprise of Song 1

After the number, they see someone approaching from off R, *and conceal themselves behind the trees*

Goody runs on R. *She is still tearful and upset. She pauses to take in her surroundings, then sits beneath a tree* L. *She drops her face into her hands and weeps*

The Demons emerge from behind their trees. They observe Goody, and slowly approach her, but not in a threatening manner

Simon runs on R. *He sees the creatures advancing on Goody. With angry cries, he rushes at them. The startled Demons scatter, and Simon chases them out in various directions*

Goody rises and makes for the exit L

Simon (*calling*) Goody — wait!

Goody stops, but keeps her back to him

I ... I had to come after you. It's a good thing I did. Those weird looking creatures were creeping up on you. They might have ...
Goody (*coldly*) You needn't have bothered. I've seen them before. They
don't mean any harm. (*She starts for the exit*)
Simon (*quickly moving towards her*) Goody ... please ...
Goody (*stopping, but still keeping her back to him*) I've already told
you. I don't want to listen to you.
Simon (*earnestly*) But I love you, Goody. You must believe that. I love
you with all of my heart!

Song 12

*Song for Simon. Its sincerity melts a little of Goody's coldness towards
him*

The Elf Cobbler peeps out from behind his tree, R, *unseen by Simon
and Goody. He listens carefully to the couple*

Goody And what about Cissie? You said you were in love with her.
Simon I know. And I genuinely thought I was. Oh, I can't explain it. I
wish I could. I really thought I was in love with her. I even took out
a whacking great loan to buy her that ring! Then — right out of the
blue — I suddenly knew it was you I truly loved. It just happened as
if — as if by magic!
Elf Cobbler (*coming out from behind his tree, and going to them*) That's
exactly what it was.

*Naturally, the couple are very surprised at his sudden and unusual
appearance*

Elf Cobbler Please forgive me for eavesdropping, but this does rather
concern me. It's about those shoes you are wearing.
Goody Oh, dear! Do they belong to you?
Elf Cobbler No. But they were in my charge for a while. I had the job of
repairing them. They belong to Septica. She's a Sorceress.
Goody A Sorceress?
Elf Cobbler Yes. And a particularly unpleasant one.
Simon (*rather sternly*) Would you mind telling us what all this is
about?
Elf Cobbler Certainly. It's about magic.
Simon ⎫
Goody ⎭ (*together*) Magic?
Elf Cobbler Yes. Those are magic shoes.

The couple look down at Goody's shoes, then start laughing

Simon (*to the Elf Cobbler, sceptically*) Is this for real?
Elf Cobbler Very real indeed. (*To Goody*) Tell me, have you made any
  wishes since you've been wearing them?
Goody I — I can't remember ...
Elf Cobbler Have you wished for something and it's actually come
  true?
Goody (*remembering*) When I first put them on I did wish for someone
  special to see me wearing them.
Elf Cobbler And?
Goody Simon came along.
Elf Cobbler Exactly!
Goody But that doesn't mean it had anything to do with magic.
Elf Cobbler Believe me, my dear, it had!
Simon I say! It could explain about my winning that two hundred
  pounds! You wished I had it to give you, and the next thing we knew
  — I'd won it in the raffle!
Goody That's true!
Simon It could also explain about my falling in love with Cissie!
Goody Yes! She bought the shoes from me. She must have found out
  they were magic and ——
Simon Wished I was in love with *her!*
Goody And then she gave them back to me, and I wished ——
Elf Cobbler (*rather impatiently*) Yes, yes! It all fits. I'll tell you more
  about it. Only not here! (*Looking about, nervously*) It isn't safe! Come
  into my workshop, and I'll explain everything. This *way*. (*He leads
  them over to his tree*)
            O, Magic trunk of magic tree,
            Open up your door for me!

There is a magical sound, and the door in the tree opens by itself

(*To Goody*) Before we go in. Please would you mind removing those
troublesome shoes and leaving them outside.

*Without hesitation, Goody removes the shoes, and puts them on the
ground beneath the tree*

Now! In you both go! (*He ushers them inside*) Mind your heads!

*Goody and Simon go into the tree. The Elf follows, shutting the door
behind him*

Cissie (*off* UR; *wailing*) *Thimon! Thimon!*

Cissie wanders into view, a bedraggled, tear-stained, and pathetic figure

(*Still wailing*) Thimon! Oooh! (*Moving forward*) Where ith he? Where ith he? Thimon!

Two of the larger and more gruesome-looking Demons emerge from behind the trees. They creep up behind Cissie. Eventually, probably responding to hints supplied by the audience, she sees the Demons. Screaming, she runs out DL. Grunting with devilish glee, the Demons shamble off in pursuit of her

Tightwad (*off* DR; *calling*) Cissie! *Cissie!*

Tightwad stomps into view, a dishevelled, disgruntled and irate figure

(*Still calling*) *Cissie! Cissie!* Bah! Where is the confounded girl? Chasing after some young fella in this filthy forest! (*Bellowing*) Cissie!! Bah! If it wasn't for her inheritance, I'd leave her here! (*He sees the shoes beneath the tree*) And look at this! (*He picks them up*) It's those shoes she was so keen on having! Just thrown on the ground! Cost me twenty pounds! Bah! Well, I'll keep 'em for meself! (*To someone in the front row*) No, not to wear! I can sell 'em at (*local market/car boot sale*)!

Tightwad stumps out DL, clutching the shoes and calling "Cissie! Cissie!" as he goes

Septica limps on from UR. She is followed by Rolo and Polo, who are dragging Molly and Teddy

Molly Listen, Mrs Septic tank — or whatever yer name is —we 'ad nothin' to do with this!
Teddy No! We're completely ignorant!
Septica *Silence!* As soon as I have found the thief who stole my precious shoes, you will both share in her hideous fate!

Cissie creeps on backwards DR. She is making terrified, whimpering noises. Septica turns and sees her

It's her! The shoe thief!

Cissie screams, turns tail, and runs out DR

After her! Don't let her get away!

Septica limps out in pursuit of Cissie

The duo releases Molly and Teddy

Rolo (*to Molly*) Now's your chance! Make a run for it!
Polo Yeah! That's what we're gonna do!

Rolo and Polo run out DL

Molly and Teddy just run round the stage in a mad panic. They run to the exit DR, *see something, and run* US *to hide behind the trees* L

Cissie runs on from DR, *yelling, being pursued by the two Demons. They chase her round the stage, then out* DL

Molly and Teddy emerge from hiding. They creep cautiously DS, *and peer off* DL

Septica enters DR *unseen by Molly and Teddy*

The audience will be shouting warnings. Taking no notice, and still looking towards DL, *Molly and Teddy creep across towards the* DR *exit. They back into the static figure of Septica, and stop dead*

Molly (*to Teddy, gulping*) Somethin' tells me we're 'avin' a close encounter of the nasty kind!

In terror, they slowly turn their heads to look. Septica snarls at them. They both yell

Molly and Teddy run out DL. *Septica limps out after them*

Rolo and Polo run across the back, from UL, *and out* UR

Tightwad stumps on from DL, *still clutching the shoes*

Tightwad (*calling as he crosses*) Cissie! Cissie!

Tightwad exits DR

The door in the tree opens, and the Elf Cobbler peeps out. After making sure the coast is clear, he comes out, then signals for Goody and Simon to follow. The tree door remains open. They move away from the tree. None of them notices that the shoes have gone

Goody (*to the Elf Cobbler*) Thank you for explaining everything to us.
Simon Yes. I still find it incredible.
Goody So do I. Just think, I was wearing magic shoes and never knew it. But they've caused so much trouble, I wish I'd left them alone.
Elf Cobbler Well, they appear to have done some good. (*With a twinkle*) They brought you two together.
Goody Yes, that's true. Without them we would never have met.
Simon (*taking her hands*) I'm not so sure about that. I think you and I were destined to meet, Goody. With or without the aid of magic shoes.
Goody (*sighing and gazing adoringly at him*) Oh, Simon!
Simon (*ditto*) Oh, Goody!

They embrace. Rather embarrassed, the Elf Cobbler looks the other way. He then gives a politic little cough

Elf Cobbler Ahhem! This is all very nice, but I really think we should attend to the matter in hand. (*Looking at the embrace*) The *other* matter in hand, I mean ... not ... er ... Ahhem!

The couple part

Simon Of course. If this Sorceress is intent on revenge, we'd better think of some way of defending ourselves.
Elf Cobbler (*shaking his head*) That would be useless. Septica has all the powers of evil magic at her disposal. You can't defend yourself against that. I suggest you do as I intend doing. Get as far away from her as possible! (*Looking about him, nervously*) And as soon as possible.
Simon It sounds like the only sensible solution.
Goody (*suddenly struck by an idea*) Wait! I have an idea! Suppose I were to put the shoes back on, and wished for Septica to disappear!
Simon Yes! (*To the Elf Cobbler*) Would that work?
Elf Cobbler (*unsure*) Well ...
Goody It's worth a try anyway! (*She runs to the tree, and discovers that the shoes are no longer there*) Oh!

Simon and the Elf Cobbler run to join Goody

Simon What's wrong?
Goody The shoes have gone!

Molly and Teddy run on L

Molly Goody! Goody! You've got to 'elp us!
Teddy We're bein' chased by a very sore Sorceress!
Molly She's gonna ... (*She suddenly notices the Elf*) Crikey! That's a big garden gnome!
Elf Cobbler (*going to the door of his tree*) Quickly! In here!
Molly And it can walk an' talk! What the ... ?
Goody There's no time to explain now, Mum! Just do as he says!

Goody and Simon go into the tree

Molly *In there?* I don't wanna catch woodworm!
Teddy (*pushing Molly towards the doorway*) Hurry up, Mum!

Molly enters the doorway — and gets stuck! There is comic business as Teddy and the Elf Cobbler manage to push her through. Teddy follows her inside. The Elf Cobbler goes in, and is just about to shut the door, when Rolo and Polo run on from L

Duo (*as they run to the tree*) Wait! Wait! Let us in!
Teddy (*poking his head out through the doorway*) What's up?
Rolo Septica knows we let you escape!
Polo And now she's after us!
Teddy (*to Elf*) Let 'em in!

Teddy disappears inside the tree

The Elf Cobbler lets the duo rush into the tree

Elf Cobbler (*to the audience*) It's a good job I had that extension built!

The Elf Cobbler goes into the tree, shutting the door behind him

Cissie runs on DL, *yelling, pursued by the two Demons. She runs to the exit* DR

Septica enters DR

Cissie pulls up short, screams, and runs back, straight into the arms of the waiting Demons. They grab her and pull her DL

The rest of the Demons emerge from behind the trees to skulk in the background

Septica limps across to the cringing Cissie. She looks down at her feet, and gives a frenzied shriek

Septica *Ahhgh!!* Where are they? Where are my precious shoes? What have you done with them?
Cissie (*in total misery*) I ... I haven't got them any more! I gave them to Goody! *The'th* got them now! *The'th* the one you want!
Septica Where is she?
Cissie In the foretht!
Septica Then I will find her!
Cissie (*relieved*) Yeth!
Septica And *you* will share in her punishment!
Cissie (*in misery again*) Oooo!
Septica Take her away!

The Demons prepare to haul the wailing Cissie out DL

Tightwad enters from DR. *He is still clutching the shoes*

Tightwad *My niece!*
Cissie *My uncle!*
Septica (*seeing them*) My shoes! (*Advancing a little towards Tightwad*) Give those shoes to me at once! They are *mine!* They belong to *me!*
Tightwad (*also advancing a little*) Oh, no, they don't! They belong to *me!* I paid twenty pounds for 'em!

At this point, Tightwad needs to be quite close to the Elf Cobbler's tree. No-one sees the door slowly opening

Septica You fool! Be warned! If you don't give me those shoes this instant something extremely unpleasant will happen to you! Give me those shoes! *They're mine!*
Tightwad (*holding the shoes aloft in one hand*) They're mine!

The Elf Cobbler suddenly appears in the now open doorway

Elf Cobbler *They're mine!*

The Elf Cobbler swiftly snatches the shoes from Tightwad's hand, disappears inside with them, and slams the door shut

Septica lets out a frenzied shriek, while Tightwad gazes at his empty hand in utter amazement

Septica (*pointing to Tightwad*) Seize him!

One of the Demons holding Cissie lumbers up, grabs the still dazed Tightwad, and hauls him DL

(*Flying at the Elf Cobbler's tree and pounding on the trunk in a furious frenzy*) Open this door, Elf! Open it at once, and give me those shoes! Open it, I say! (*She pounds on the trunk*)

The voice of the Elf Cobbler is heard. It appears to be echoing from inside the tree. NOTE: An offstage microphone should be used for this with an amplifier concealed in the tree

Elf Cobbler (*voice-over; sternly*) Don't do that! Stop it! Stop it at once!

Septica reacts to the volume of the voice, and stops her pounding

(*Politely*) Thank you. We don't want to give the squirrels a headache, do we?

Septica Listen to me, you interfering little garden ornament! If you don't open this door at once, I will conjure up a mighty thunderbolt. It will blast this tree of yours — and everything in it — to atoms!

Elf Cobbler (*voice-over; still politely*) I see. And does that also include your precious pair of shoes?

This stumps Septica, and she gives a frustrated roar

(*With a little chuckle*) I didn't think so. I have a proposition to put to you. Are you listening?

Septica (*with a snarl*) Yes!

Elf Cobbler (*voice-over*) If you promise to let these people go free and unharmed, and never to bother any of them again, I will let you have your shoes back. Do you agree to do that?

Septica limps up and down, in a fever of indecision

Well? I'm waiting for your answer. Do you agree?

Septica (*with a grudging snarl*) Yes!

Elf Cobbler (*voice-over*) Do you promise?
Septica (*impatiently*) Yes! Yes! *I promise!* Just give me my shoes!
Elf Cobbler (*off*) Very well. We're coming out.

The door in the tree opens. The Elf Cobbler comes out, carrying the shoes. The others file out behind him

Septica (*to the Elf Cobbler*) Give me those! (*She snatches the shoes from him, and hugs them*) At last! At last! My lovely, comfy shoes! (*She hastily removes the shoes she is wearing, and throws them offstage or to one of the Demons. She then puts on the other pair, and gives a great sigh of relief*) Ahh! Bliss! Utter bliss! Ahhhh!
Molly Right! Now she's 'appy, we can all go 'ome!

Molly and the others prepare to leave

Septica (*snarling*) Not so fast! (*She signals to the Demons*)

With fiendish grunts, the Demons quickly surround Molly and the others, and herd them to R. The two Demons with Tightwad and Cissie drag them over to join the others. Septica remains C, laughing her fiendish laugh. There are cries of protest and confusion from the others

Septica You poor, deluded fools! Did you really think I was going to let you get away with this!
Molly (*to the others, scared*) Ooh! Somethin' tells me we're not gonna be watchin' (*TV soap*) tonight!
Elf Cobbler (*to Septica*) But ... But you made me a promise.
Septica (*scornfully*) Ha! A promise to a puny Elf! That means nothing to me! I am Septica, the Sorceress! (*She gives another burst of fiendish laughter*) Hee! Hee! Hee! However, there is one promise I *do* intend to keep! I promise that you will all suffer — as you have never suffered before! (*More fiendish laughter*) Hee! Hee! Hee!

The others react with fear and foreboding

Simon What are you going to do to us?
Teddy (*trembling*) D-Does it involve pain? I'm allergic to that!
Septica You are all responsible, in one way or another, for keeping my precious shoes from me! For that you shall receive the ultimate punishment — *death!*

There are wails and lamentations from the others

With the return of these shoes the full power of my awesome magic has
been restored! Now I can give you a truly magnificent and spectacular
death! Prepare to die! *(More fiendish laughter)* Hee! Hee! Hee!

*There is a blinding flash of lightning, followed by a tremendous clap
of thunder. The Lighting becomes dark and spooky. Weird, unearthly
sounds fill the air. Sinister music plays under. The others cling to each
other in terror*

(*To the audience, menacingly*) And when I've dealt with them, it will
be my enormous pleasure to deal with *you!* Hee! Hee! Hee!

*Septica sweeps L, laughing. (Note: She needs to be fairly close to the
wings for her sudden disappearance) An eerie spotlight comes up on
her*

Septica   My demonic powers I mean to use,
                 On those who stole my precious shoes!
                 The consequences they shall bear,
                 Of helping themselves to *my* footwear!
   (Pointing to the terrified group, she casts her evil spell)
                 By the powers of darkness invested in me,
                 I condemn you to die — in slow agony!

*There is a blinding flash, followed by a complete Black-out. Magical
sounds and music are heard. There are confused cries from the others*

   Septica exits

The Demons retreat into the background

*The Lights come up. The general lighting is now brighter than ever
before, turning the forest into a much pleasanter-looking place. The
magical sounds and music fade out. Everyone is dazed and amazed;
everyone except the Elf Cobbler, that is*

Molly Hey! Where's Nightmare Nellie gone?
Elf Cobbler I knew she couldn't be trusted. That's why I took the
precaution of switching the shoes.

*There are puzzled exclamations from the others, i.e. "What's he mean?"
"What's he talking about?" etc., etc.*

Elf Cobbler Let me explain. I swapped Septica's shoes for another pair of magic shoes I already had in my workshop. They belong to a Good Fairy who brought them in to be repaired last week. I knew *her* shoes could only be used for casting *good* spells. I also knew that if a person tried to cast an *evil* spell while wearing them, the spell would automatically rebound on that person. And that is exactly what happened to Septica. Fortunately the shoes are identical in size and appearance, so she never noticed the switch.

Teddy That's lucky!

Molly (*with a wink to the audience*) That's more than lucky!

Simon (*to the Elf Cobbler*) Well, your quick thinking certainly saved us from a very nasty fate. (*He shakes the Elf Cobbler's hand*) Thank you.

Goody Yes. We owe you our lives. Thank you. (*She kisses the Elf Cobbler on the cheek*)

The Elf Cobbler shows embarrassed delight. All the others express their gratitude

Goody What happened to Septica's shoes?

Elf Cobbler Here they are! (*He takes the shoes from the pocket of his apron*) I'll have to give them to the Good Fairy in return for the ones that ... er ... went up in smoke, as it were.

Goody Before you do, could I put them on for one last time?

Elf Cobbler Do you intend making a wish?

Goody Just one.

Elf Cobbler Oh, very well. (*He gives the shoes to Goody*)

Goody puts the shoes on

Molly A couple of million each should be enough! We won't spend it all at once.

Teddy No. You know the old saying: a fool and his money are soon parted at Woolies! (*Or local shop*)

Molly Teddy?

Teddy Yes, Mum?

Molly I've got an old saying for *you!* It's this! Shut yer mouth and give yer ar...

Goody (*cutting in*) I'm ready to make my wish now.

There is silence as she moves to the centre to make her wish

I wish for everyone to be happy, and to be kind to one another!

There is a magical effect with a Lighting change and magical music, etc. As soon as normal service is resumed, everyone hugs, kisses and shakes hands with everyone else. The Demons come forward to shake hands and hug the others

The Villagers enter and join in

There is comic business as Cissie hugs Teddy, and Tightwad hugs Molly

Cissie Teddy, would you like to take me out?
Teddy (*delighted*) You bet!
Cissie I promith I won't wear thith thilly hat! (*She throws the offending article away*)
Tightwad Mrs Coddle ... er ... Molly. I've decided to let you live at the cottage for as long as you like — rent free.
Molly Oooh!
Tightwad On the condition that I can come and visit you whenever I feel like it. (*He nudges her and winks*)
Molly (*playing up to him*) Oh! You saucy old saucepot, you! (*She gives him a hefty nudge*)
Tightwad (*moving away to address the entire ensemble*) I think a celebration is called for! You are all invited to my house this evening for a party! (*He takes out his wallet on the chain, and waves it*) No expense spared!

General rejoicing! Molly grabs the wallet, and uses the chain to pull Tightwad back to her. Goody removes the shoes, and gives them to the Elf Cobbler. Taking out the ring box, Simon offers the ring to Goody. She takes it and slips it on her finger. Everyone cheers as the young lovers embrace. They all go into a joyful song and dance

Song 13

Song and dance for Principals and Chorus. At the end of the song, the Tabs close or a frontcloth is lowered

Before the party

Tabs, or the front cloth used in ACT II, SCENE 3

Teddy bounces on DR, *and waves to the audience*

Teddy Hallo, folks! Hi, kids! Well, what d'you think of that, eh? Cissie fancies me! And she wants me to take her to the party tonight! Isn't that great! It only goes to prove the old saying: everything comes to he who waits for a pig in a poke!

Molly rushes on DR

Molly (*calling*) Teddy? ... Teddy? Oh, there you are! (*She sees the audience, and waves*) Oh, hallo, you lot! Listen, Teddy. I've got a *huge* problem!
Teddy Yeah! I can see it from here, Mum!
Molly It's Titus!
Teddy I bet it is!
Molly Look, will you stop messin' about! This is serious! I'm sure Titus Tightwad is gonna propose to me at the party tonight! Oh! I'm a right flapdoodle about it! I mean — (*to the audience, acting coy*) what is a young girl to do?
Teddy Let's find one and ask her!
Molly I just know 'e's gonna ask for my hand in marriage! Do I give it to 'im?
Teddy That depends on how much he's gonna put in it! Since Goody made that wish old Titus isn't a miser any more, is he? Just think, Mum, all his lovely loot could be yours!
Molly (*mulling it over*) I know ... (*Then, O.T.T tragic*) But, is it right? Can I be bought with an old man's gold? Can I be a bird in a gilded cage? Can I become — *a kept woman*? (*Down to earth*) You bet I can! (*To Teddy*) Now that's sorted, what 'ave you got planned for our mates out there before they go?
Teddy Something really special, Mum! (*He whispers in her ear*)
Molly Oooh! Lovely! And I bet they thought they'd got away with it too! (*To the audience, mischievously*) I'm goin' now. I just can't stand to see grown men cry! Bye! Bye!

Molly exits DL, *waving*

Rolo enters DR, *Polo enters* DL. *They each carry a placard with the blank side facing the audience. Note: the following is only a suggestion. A different routine can be substituted if desired. Whatever is chosen it should end with an audience participation song*

Teddy (c; *to the audience*) Now! We want you all to play ——

There is a fanfare from the piano/band

The humming game!
Rolo It's very simple. (*Indicating the right side of the audience*) *This* side will hum the tune of a song.
Polo (*indicating the left side*) And *this* side has to guess what the song is!
Teddy Then *that* side hums a song, and *this* side has to guess what it is. Don't worry, Gran! It won't be anything by (*current pop group*)!
Rolo Now, you mustn't *sing* the words! All you have to do is hum.
Polo That should be easy for some of 'em! (*Jokingly holding his nose*) Phew!!
Teddy Right! Let's get started! (*To Rolo*) Show your side the name of the song they've got to hum!

The house lights come up, and Rolo goes down into the auditorium. He holds up his placard to the right hand side of audience without letting the other side see. It should be a well-known song. There are by-play and ad-libs as he prevents them from revealing the name of the song, etc.

Are you ready? Right then! On the count of three you start humming! One — two — three!

There is comic business as Rolo and his side have fun attempting to hum the song. After a while, Teddy stops them

Right! Thank you! Thank you! That should be enough!

Rolo returns to the stage, keeping his placard concealed

(*To Polo*) Now! Who on your side wants to guess the identity of the song?

Polo invites various members to guess. After some comic by-play and ad-libs, the correct answer is given. Rolo holds up his placard. Teddy leads everyone in applause. The whole humming business is then repeated by Polo and his side of the audience. The routine can be repeated as desired. It should end by both sides of the audience actually singing one of their songs against each other. Song sheets can be lowered, or Rolo and Polo can bring them on from the wings

Song 14

House song for Teddy, Rolo, Polo and the audience

If desired, children can be brought up from the audience to participate. They are returned to their seats, and the house lights go down

Teddy and the others run out, waving goodbye to the audience

The Lights fade to Blackout

The frontcloth is flown out

SCENE 6

The Grand Finale

There is a special finale setting, or the forest scene can be used with the addition of a triumphal arch and flower garlands, etc.

There is a fanfare. The Lights come up brightly. Bouncy music plays

All enter for the finale walkdown and bows

The last to enter are Goody and Simon, magnificently attired

Goody The time has come to say farewell.
Simon Our tale is now complete.
Septica They double-crossed me with that spell!
Polo Oh, go and — soak yer feet!
Elf Cobbler Those magic shoes caused quite a fuss.
Teddy They made us look a wally!
Cissie (*spraying Teddy*) But thingth have turned out nithe for uth.
Rolo Please give that man a brolly!
Tightwad I'd like to spend a pound or two.
Molly Ooh! Spend until you burst!
Tightwad (*to Molly*) I have a bundle just for *you*.
Molly Let's see yer money first!

Teddy We hope you have enjoyed yourselves.
Molly Our aim was to amuse.
Goody A fond farewell to all of you ——
All From Goody and her shoes!

Finale Song 15 (or Reprise)

CURTAIN

FURNITURE AND PROPERTY LIST

Further dressing may be added at the Director's discretion

ACT 1
SCENE 1

On stage: Forest backcloth
            Tree, undergrowth and creeper wings
            Tree with concealed practical door in trunk

Off stage: Pair of magic shoes (**Elf Cobbler**)
            Greenery (**Molly**)

Personal: **Goody**: shoes

SCENE 2

On stage: Tabs or frontcloth

Off stage: Hat with flowers, etc (**Cissie**)

Personal: **Tightwad**: purse on chain containing banknotes
            Goody: magic shoes

SCENE 3

On stage: Village backcloth
            Village wings
            Molly's cottage with practical door

Off stage: Raffle ticket and wad of bank notes (**Villager**)

Personal: **Goody**: magic shoes
            Cissie: shoes
            Tightwad: rent demand

ACT II

Scene 1

On stage:	Tabs or frontcloth. As ACT I, Scene 2
Off stage:	Six large cards with captions (**Teddy**)
	On 1st card: "THE STORY SO FAR" / "POOR GOODY. AHH!"
	On 2nd card: "HER POOR MUM" / "HER HANDSOME BROTHER. HURRAY!"
	On 3rd card: "THE WICKED LANDLORD. BOO! HISS!" / "HIS NASTY NIECE! BOO!"
	On 4th card: "THE HERO"/ "THE ALSO RANS"
	On 5th card: "BOO! HISS!" / "HURRAY!"
	On 6th card: "A QUICK RECAP"
	Huge card. On it: "CUT!!"/ "BACK TO THE PLOT!" (**Teddy**)
Personal:	**Cissie**: Magic shoes

Scene 2

On stage:	Village setting. As ACT I, Scene 3
Off stage:	Nil
Personal:	**Cissie**: magic shoes

Scene 3

On stage:	Tabs or frontcloth. As ACT II, Scene 1
Off stage:	Box with ring (**Simon**)
Personal:	**Cissie**: magic shoes

Scene 4

On stage:	Forest setting. As ACT I, Scene 1
Off stage:	Second pair of magic shoes (**Elf Cobbler**)
	First pair of magic shoes (in pocket of apron) (**Elf Cobbler**)
Personal:	**Goody**: magic shoes
	Septica: Shoes
	Tightwad: Purse on chain
	Simon: Box with ring

Scene 5

On stage:	Tabs or frontcloth. As ACT II, Scene 3

Off stage: Placard with name of song **(Rolo)**
                Placard with name of song **(Polo)**
                Song sheets **(Rolo and Polo or Stage Management)**
                Sweets for Audience **(Rolo and Polo)**

SCENE 6
GRAND FINALE

On stage: Special finale setting, or the forest scene with the addition of a
                triumphal arch, garlands, etc.

LIGHTING PLOT

Property fittings required: nil
Various interior and exterior settings

ACT I, SCENE 1

To open: Spooky lighting

Cue 1	**Rolo** enters Brighten general lighting	(Page 1)
Cue 2	**Septica** enters Dim general lighting	(Page 1)
Cue 3	**Septica** exits Brighten general lighting	(Page 3)
Cue 4	**Teddy** and **Molly** sing SONG 2 *Follow spot*	(Page 8)
Cue 5	End of SONG 2 *Take out spot*	(Page 8)
Cue 6	**Goody** and the **Villagers** sing SONG 3 *Follow spot*	(Page 9)
Cue 7	End of SONG 3 *Take out spot*	(Page 9)
Cue 8	**Goody**: " ...would instantly fall in love with me." *Magical lighting effect*	(Page 13)
Cue 9	**Simon** enters *Fade out magical effect and return to previous general lighting*	(Page 13)
Cue 10	**Simon** and **Goody** sing SONG 4 *Romantic lighting with follow spot*	(Page 14)
Cue 11	End of SONG 4 *Take out spot and return to previous general lighting*	(Page 14)

| *Cue* 12 | **Rolo** and **Polo** exit | (Page 21) |
| | *Dim general lighting. Eerie follow spot on* **Septica** | |

Cue 13	**Septica** exits	(Page 21)
	Take out spot and return to strange	
	and spooky general lighting	

| *Cue* 14 | End of Reprise of SONG 1 | (Page 21) |
| | *Fade lights to Black-out* | |

ACT I, SCENE 2

To open: Bright general exterior lighting

| *Cue* 15 | **Cissie** sings SONG 5 | (Page 27) |
| | *Follow spot* | |

| *Cue* 16 | End of SONG 5 | (Page 27) |
| | *Take out spot* | |

| *Cue* 17 | **Rolo** and **Polo** exit | (Page 31) |
| | *Fade lights to black-out* | |

ACT I, SCENE 3

To open: Bright general exterior lighting

| *Cue* 18 | **Villagers** sing SONG 6 | (Page 31) |
| | *Follow spot* | |

| *Cue* 19 | End of SONG 6 | (Page 31) |
| | *Take out spot* | |

Cue 20	**Goody**: "I wish you had as well, Simon."	(Page 37)
	Magical effect. Allow time for reactions, then fade out	
	magical effect and return to previous general lighting	

| *Cue* 21 | **Villagers** sing SONG 7 | (Page 38) |
| | *Follow spot* | |

| *Cue* 22 | End of SONG 7 | (Page 38) |
| | *Take out spot* | |

Cue 23	**Cissie**: " ... and not with Goody!"	(Page 44)
	Magical lighting effect, dark and sinister	
	with thunder and lightning	

Cue 24	**Molly**: "(*TV weather presenter*) didn't forecast this!" *Fade out magical effect and return to previous general lighting*	(Page 44)
Cue 25	End of SONG 8; tableau *Fade lights to black-out*	(Page 46)

ACT II, SCENE 1

To open: General exterior lighting

Cue 26	**Teddy** shows caption: "POOR GOODY. AHH!" *Flickering light effect. (Not strobe)*	(Page 47)
Cue 27	**Teddy** shows caption: "A QUICK RECAP" *Increase speed of flickering light*	(Page 49)
Cue 28	**Teddy** shows caption: "CUT!" *Stop flickering light effect abruptly; return to general lighting*	(Page 49)
Cue 29	**Rolo** and **Polo** exit *Dim general lighting. Eerie follow spot on* **Septica**	(Page 52)
Cue 30	**Septica** exits *Fade lights to Black-out*	(Page 53)

ACT II, SCENE 2

To open: Bright general exterior lighting

Cue 31	**Molly**, **Teddy** and the **Villagers** sing SONG 9 *Follow spot*	(Page 53)
Cue 32	End of SONG 9 *Take out spot*	(Page 53)
Cue 33	**Goody** sings SONG 10 *Dim general lighting. Follow spot on* **Goody**	(Page 55)
Cue 34	End of SONG 10 *Take out spot and return to previous general lighting*	(Page 55)
Cue 35	End of reprise of SONG 10 *Fade lights to black-out*	(Page 58)

ACT II, SCENE 3

To open: Bright general exterior lighting

| Cue 36 | **Teddy** and **Cissie** sing SONG 11 | (Page 60) |
| | *Follow spot* | |

| Cue 37 | End of SONG 11 | (Page 60) |
| | *Take out spot* | |

| Cue 38 | **Goody**: "I wish I had the love of Simon back as well." | (Page 64) |
| | *Magical lighting effect* | |

Cue 39	As **Simon** enters	(Page 65)
	Fade out magical effect	
	and return to previous general lighting	

| Cue 40 | **Septica** exits | (Page 70) |
| | *Fade to black-out* | |

ACT II, SCENE 4

To open: Strange and spooky general exterior lighting

| Cue 41 | **Goody** enters | (Page 70) |
| | *Brighten general lighting* | |

| Cue 42 | **Simon** sings SONG 12 | (Page 71) |
| | *Dim general lighting. Follow spot on* **Simon** | |

| Cue 43 | End of SONG 12 | (Page 71) |
| | *Take out spot and return to previous general lighting* | |

| Cue 44 | **Elf Cobbler**: "This way." | (Page 72) |
| | *Spot on door in tree* | |

| Cue 45 | The **Elf Cobbler** goes into the tree and shuts the door | (Page 72) |
| | *Take out spot* | |

Cue 46	**Septica**: "Hee! Hee! Hee!"	(Page 80)
	Blinding flash of lightning;	
	general lighting becomes dark and sinister	

| Cue 47 | **Septica** sweeps L | (Page 80) |
| | *Eerie spotlight comes up on* **Septica** | |

| Cue 48 | **Septica**: " — in slow agony" | (Page 80) |
| | *Blinding flash followed by black-out* | |

Cue 49	**Septica** exits and the **Demons** retreat *Bring up bright general exterior lighting*	(Page 80)
Cue 50	**Goody**: " ... and to be kind to one another." *Magical lighting effect*	(Page 82)
Cue 51	When ready *Cut magical effect and return to previous general lighting*	(Page 82)
Cue 52	**Principals** and **Chorus** sing SONG 13 *Follow spot*	(Page 82)
Cue 53	End of SONG 13 *Take out spot*	(Page 82)

ACT II SCENE 5

To open: General lighting

Cue 54	**Teddy**: " ... the song they've got to hum!" *Bring up house lights*	(Page 84)
Cue 55	**Teddy**, **Rolo** and **Polo** sing SONG 14 *Spot on song sheets*	(Page 85)
Cue 56	The children return to the audience *Take out house lights and spot*	(Page 85)
Cue 57	**Teddy** and the others exit *Fade to black-out*	(Page 85)

ACT II SCENE 6

To open: Darkness

| *Cue* 58 | Fanfare
Bring up bright general lighting | (Page 85) |

EFFECTS PLOT

ACT I

Cue 1   As CURTAIN rises   (Page 1)
           Eerie sounds. Ground mist

Cue 2   End of SONG 1   (Page 1)
           Fade out eerie sounds

Cue 3   **Goody**: " ... who would instantly fall in love with me." (Page 13)
           Magical sounds

Cue 4   **Simon** enters   (Page 13)
           Fade out magical sounds

Cue 5   **Septica** exits   (Page 21)
           Eerie sounds. Ground mist

Cue 6   **Goody**: "I wish you had as well, Simon."   (Page 37)
           Magical sounds. Allow time for reactions,
              then fade out magical sounds

Cue 7   **Cissie**: "I wi'th that Thimon was in love with *me*   (Page 44)
              and not with Goody."
           Eerie magical sounds

Cue 8   **Molly**: "(TV weather presenter) didn't forecast this!"   (Page 44)
           Fade out magical sounds

ACT II

Cue 9   **Goody**: "I wish I had the love of Simon back as well."   (Page 64)
           Magical sounds

Cue 10   **Simon** enters   (Page 65)
           Fade out magical sounds

Cue 11   To open SCENE 4   (Page 70)
           Eerie sounds and ground mist

Cue 12   As GOODY enters   (Page 70)
           Fade out eerie sounds

Cue 13	**Elf Cobbler**: "Open up your door for me!" *Magical sound*	(Page 72)
Cue 14	**Septica** pounds on the trunk of the tree *Switch on offstage microphone for* **Elf Cobbler**	(Page 78)
Cue 15	**Septica**: "Hee! Hee! Hee!" Lightning *Tremendous clap of thunder; weird, unearthly sounds*	(Page 80)
Cue 16	Black-out *Magical sounds*	(Page 80)
Cue 17	The Lights come up *Fade magical sounds*	(Page 80)

COPYRIGHT MUSIC

The notice printed below on behalf of the Performing Right Society should be carefully read if any copyright music is used in this play.

The permission of the owner of the performing rights in copyright music must be obtained before any public performance may be given, whether in conjunction with a play or sketch or otherwise, and this permission is just as necessary for amateur performances as for professional. The majority of copyright musical works (other than oratorios, musical plays and similar dramatico-musical works) are controlled in the British Commonwealth by the PERFORMING RIGHT SOCIETY LTD, 29-33 Berners Street, London W1P 4AA.

The Society's practice is to issue licences authorizing the use of its repertoire to the proprietors of premises at which music is publicly performed, or, alternatively, to the organizers of musical entertainments, but the Society does not require payment of fees by performers as such. Producers or promoters of plays, sketches, etc., at which music is to be performed, during or after the play or sketch, should ascertain whether the premises at which their performances are to be given are covered by a licence issued by the Society, and if they are not, should make application to the Society for particulars as to the fee payable.

A separate and additional licence from PHONOGRAPHIC PERFORMANCES LTD, 1 Upper James Street, London W1R 3HG, is needed whenever commercial recordings are used.

CPSIA information can be obtained
at www.ICGtesting.com
Printed in the USA
FSOW02n2305081216
28358FS